A ROLE OF BOON (VARADĀNA) IN SOME UPANIṢADIC STORIES

A ROLE OF BOON (VARADĀNA) IN SOME UPANIṢADIC STORIES

By

Dr. Vaijayanti D. Shete

BHARATIYA KALA PRAKASHAN
DELHI (INDIA)

First Published : 2000

Published by **C.P. Gautam**
BHARATIYA KALA PRAKASHAN
3421-A, IInd Floor, Narang Colony, Tri Nagar,
Delhi-110035. Phone : 7153083

ISBN : 81-86050-55-8

Laser Type Setting by
A-ONEGRAPHICS
X-4, Gali-2, Brahmapuri, Delhi-110053
Phone : 218 3470

Printed at
Santosh Offset
40, Anand Nagar, Inderlok, Delhi
Phones : 511 6763, 511 7390

ब्रह्मार्पणं ब्रह्म हविर्ब्रह्माग्नौ ब्रह्मणा हुतम्।
ब्रह्मैव तेन गन्तव्यं—ब्रह्मकर्मसमाधिना।।

—श्रीमद्भगवद्गीता 4.24

CONTENTS

PREFACE

This research work presents a critical survey of the Upaniṣadic stories with special reference to varadana aspect. Upaniṣadic literature furnish matter from various philosophical problems. They reflect on the religio-socio-philosophical development of the ancient period. They are an epitome of the cultural philosophical life. Dominance of the Brāhmaṇas is an important factor in the social build up. Upaniṣadas also mark the existence of enlightened group and highly educated personalities, those, actively participates in unraveling the mystery of the creation of the world. Neverthless the present work represents all-sided efforts for high-lighting the progress and development in the network of philosophical pursuits. The beauty of this vast literature lies in its eternal freshness and novelty. To each and every mind this great work reveals a new meaning and a new a charm. Some legends possess historical value. This monograph offers a new approach to the study of Upaniṣadas. They have always been the pivot of Indian religious art.

I hope that this new edition will stimulate interest in the study of the Upaniṣadas.

All that nor remains is the pleasant opportunity of thanks giving to all those who helped me in the process of preparing this work. I am grateful to my teacher and guide Prof. Dr. S.G. Kantawala, Ex. Director of Oriental Institute, Baroda, also Prof. & Head, Deptt. of Sanskrit, Pali and Prakrit, Faculty of Arts, M.S. University of Baroda for valuabe guidance and suggestion. Though he was very much busy in his official duties he spared his precious time in going through the whole thesis critically with keen interest.

I am also grateful to D.D. Mahurkar, Ex. Head Department of Linguistics, Faculty of Arts, M.S.U. who constantly encouraged me to complete my work.

Pitr, Matr, rna and Bhatr rna on me is so much that I could not express my feelings without whose help and advice, this work has not seen this delightful day.

Finally I express my sincere thanks to my husband Dilip Shete, Director of Water Resources & Management Institute, M.S.U., Baroda, who constantly appreciated my efforts and pursued me to get the work published.

I mention with regards B.P. Pandya, Research Officer in Oriental Institute, Baroda for finding out the modern map of Mathuranagari which is attached with this thesis.

At the last I am thankful to Prof. Dr. M.L.Wadekar and Dr. S.Y. Wakankar for their kind co-operation and good wishes.

10th July 2000
VADODARA

Dr. Vaijayanti D. Shete

ABBREVIATIONS

1. AA — Aitareya Āraṇyaka
2. AB — Aitareya Brāhmaṇa
3. ASS — Anandashrama Sanskrit Series
4. AV — Atharvaveda
5. BG — Bhagavad Gītā
6. BHP — Bhāgavata Purāṇa
7. BORI — Bhandarkar Oriental Research Institute
8. BRP — Brahmāṇḍa Purāṇa
9. BRU — Bṛhadāraṇyaka Upaniṣad
10. CHU — Chāndogya Upaniṣad
11. Comm — Commentary
11a. GK — Gauḍapadakārikā
12. GU — Gopālottara Tāpinī Upaniṣad
13. HDS — History of Dharma Shastra
14. HIL — History of Indian Literature
15. HIP — History of the Indian Philosophy
16. HOS — Harvard Oriental Series
17. JAUB — Jaiminiya Upaniṣad Brāhmaṇa
18. JGRI — Journal of the Ganganath Jha Research Institute
19. JUB — Journal of the University of Bombay
20. KAB — Kauṣitaki Brāhmaṇa
21. KATU — Kaṭhopaniṣad
22. KAU — Kauṣitaki Upaniṣad
23. KLU — Kaivalyopaniṣad
24. M — Madvācārya
25. MAIU — Maitreya Upaniṣad of Sāmaveda
26. MAU — Maitrāyani Upaniṣad

27. MbH — Mahābhārata
28. MP — Matsya Purāṇa
29. MNU — Māṇḍukya Upaniṣad
30. MU — Muṇḍaka Upaniṣad
31. N — Nimbārkācārya
32. PU — Praṇavopaniṣad
33. R — Rāmāyaṇa
34. Rg — Raṅgarāmānuja
35. RTU — Rāmottaratāpinī Upaniṣad
36. RV — Rigveda
37. Ś — Śaṅkarācārya
38. Sāy. — Sāyaṇa
39. SB — Śatapatha Brāhmaṇa
40. SBE — Sacred Book of the East
41. ŚBH — Śāṅkarbhāṣya
42. SBH — Sacred Book of the Hindus
43. SV — Sāmaveda
44. TA — Taittiriya Āraṇyaka
45. TAB — Tāṇḍyamaha Brāhmaṇa
46. TB — Taittiriya Brāhmaṇa
47. TS — Taittiriya Saṁhitā
48. UP — Upaniṣad
49. UPS — Upaniṣads
50. V — Vallabhācārya
51. VAP — Vāyu Purāṇa
52. VP — Viṣṇu Purāṇa
53. YV — Yajurveda

SYNOPSIS

Importance and Methodology

The Modern age is an age of scientific progress and scientists try to approach the different problems or try to explain them from a scientific point of view. It is quite understandable that the scientific approaches or explanations may be known to some or some may not be known to many. It is also a common experience that a very common man is not generally interested in the scientific explanations of the things, he does every day or the things that take place around him every day. In the society there is also another group of people who is sceptic or have a keen desire to understand even the very ordinary and common things in life around them viz. belief, conventions, customs or accidental happenings etc. from a scientific point of view, or from the extra-superstition point of view. This may get an expression either in an absolutely scientific way or from a religious point of view. In the latter case, it may be expressed by saying "favour" or "grace" of a spiritual person or the deity. And this grace may be in the form of a blessing or a boon. A diety or person is pleased with a devotee and being pleased, he grants a boon to him or her that his/her wish will be fulfilled. Sometimes the displeasure of the deity or a person leads to the curse. Sometimes the curse is disguised in a boon and when the displeasure is rectified then after the curse is revised into the boon.

The idea of 'Varadāna' (boon) is met with in the Vedic, Epic, and Purāṇic and classical literature. From the study of the ancient Indian literature it appears that the boon may be a result either due to the grace or the blessing of a deity or a person and the devotee asks for his/her desired object. Sometimes the devotee leaves the desired to be chosen to the deity or the person concerned for himself/herself. Sometimes these factors may be in permutation and combination.

In the upaniṣads we come across many stories, myths and legends. Some of which have a boon as the motif or a starting point for the development of the story and expounding the philosophical doctrines.

There are works like "Stories and Dialogues". The book is a collection of the some stories from the upaniṣads in which Diwakar summarises the theme of the stories. Still the stories remained to be studied as Diwakar have not studied them from the point of view which we have under-consideration. Moreover a well-known scholar late P.B. Gajendragadkar[2] deals with the Īśa and Ken Ups. He has explained these Ups. with the help of the five commentators but he has not dealt with the story element and the boon bearing.

Thus it may be observed that the Upaniṣads have been studied by different scholars from several points of view, e.g. philosophical, educational, social etc. but the study of the boon-based stories in the Upaniṣads is desideratum. The scholars have touched these stories in the above said point of view but they have not examined the stories from the point of view which are under consideration. Hence it is proposed to study the problem of the boons and stories connected there with an analytical and critical point of view in the present book. The selection of the topic provides the reader a full idea in which the vedic people lived and moved, progressed and formed their clear, constant principles and how they were well-advanced in the spiritual life.

Herein the stories from major and minor upaniṣads are

taken up for study. The present study reveals that a boon is utilised for several purposes in the upaniṣadic stories e.g. The main purpose of the boon based stories is to expound the philosophical doctrines. Once the ṛṣi or the person concerned has arrived it the question comes naturally how to attain it and so the path, the ways and means to realise the Brahman, rituals, tapas etc. which can be considered the secondary purposes, are stated in the stories. Similarly the moral and ethical values are taught in these stories. The teaching of the Brahman as the highest knowledge may help an aspirant to proceed on the spiritual path. While doing a detailed discussion of the Highest Truth, the Upaniṣads show how the purity of mind, restraint over body and mind, sanctity, cleanliness, tapas and effect on every thought in the life of a aspirant. All these qualities play an important role in spiritual progress.

In these stories the technique of dialogue is used to develop and explain the philosophical thoughts. The genesis of the boon-motif is traceable to Saṁhitās and Brāhmaṇas. The boon-motif is found in Purāṇic religion and literature also. For the proper understanding of this concept and to understand its origin, growth and development we have taken into consideration relevant portions of Saṁhitās, Brāhmaṇas, Epics and Purāṇas even though over prime emphasis is on the Upaniṣads.

The relevant upaniṣadic portion is also examined in the light of the interpretations of the five great ācāryas viz. Śaṅkara, Rāmānuja, Madhva, Vallabha and Nimbārka and other commentators and ancient as well as modern critics.

The study is presented in the following five Chapters :

Chapter I—Concept of Boon (Vara) :—

It discusses the meaning of the word 'vara' from Saṁhitās to Purāṇas.

The Saṁhitās do present very few aspects of this concept of 'Vara'. We get some glimpses of the earlier interpretation quoted by the term 'Varam-Vṛṇṣva, Vṛṇute, avṛni etc. in the Vedas. That is to say in the Saṁhitās the word occurs in its nominal and verbal forms. In this context the Brāhmaṇas and Āraṇyakas are very useful. From Brāhmaṇas and onwards we have stories connected with the Varadāna theme. They explain a short-story like description by denoting the term "Varam-Vṛṇai" or other; over and above the occurance of the nominal forms of the vocable Vara. The stories are told in a very brief form; they do not describe it thoroughly. Some of the stories from the Epics are taken into account to examine the nature, style and development of Vara (o-dāna). The Purāṇas consist many ancient legends which are closely connected with Vedic Phenomena. That is why the Purāṇas are also taken into the consideration to examine the growth of the concept of Vara. The Purāṇas throw more light on the concept of Vara. All the Purāṇas are not taken up for the comparison but the five ancient e.g. Viṣṇu, Vāyu, Brahmāṇḍa, Matsya and Bhāgavata are taken while discussing the meaning of the vocable 'Vara'. Some of the stories are referred to in this Chapter.

Thus the Chapter studies the genesis of the concept of 'Vara' from the Vedic literature to the Purāṇic literature.

Chapter II—Conspectous and Brief Summary :—

Section I :

Upaniṣads have propounded important metaphysical doctrines sometimes through stories which have a boon-motif. The Upaniṣadic seers adopt a conversational style while introducing the boon-motif for expounding the doctrines. This Chapter deals with the following dialogues :—

1. Chāndogya Upaniṣad 5.3.6
2. Bṛhadāraṇyaka Upaniṣad 6.2.1-5

3. Bṛhadāraṇyaka Upaniṣad 1.3.28
4. Bṛhadāraṇyaka Upaniṣad 4.3.1.
5. Kaṭha Upaniṣad
6. Kauṣitaki Upaniṣad 1.1
7. Kauṣitaki Upaniṣad 3.1
8. Maitrāyaṇi Upaniṣad 1.2
9. Rāmottaratāpinī Upaniṣad.
10. Gopālottara-tāpniyopaniṣad.
11. Kaivalopaniṣad.
12. Maitreya of Sāmaveda Upaniṣad.
13. Praṇava Upaniṣad.

Section II :

Herein the contents of the above-mentioned dialogues are given. They deal with either Pañcāgnividyā or Paryaṅka vidyā or Brahmavidyā or other spiritual questions relating to the soul or means for acquiring Brahman etc. In the dialogues the light is thrown on the two paths leading a man to ascend up or to descend down. Moreover the waking, sleep and deep sleep conditions are dealt in relation with the Ātman, the highest truth.

Chapter III—Characterization

In the stories under discussion the following characters are met with :—

1. In Chāndogya 5.3.6—Śvetaketu, Āruṇi Gautama and Pravāhaṇa Jaivali;
2. In Bṛhadāraṇya 6.2.1-5 Āruṇi, Śvetaketu, Pravāhaṇa Jaivali;
3. In Bṛhadāraṇayaka 4.3.1 Janaka and Yājñavalkya;
4. In Kauṣitaki 1.1 Āruṇi and Citra Gārgyāyaṇi;
5. In Kauṣitaki 3.1. Indra and Pratardan;
6. In Kaṭha—Yama and Naciketas;
7. In Maitrāyaṇi—King Bṛhadratha and Śākāyanya;

8. In Rāmottaratāpini— Rāma and Śiva;
9. In Gopālottaratāpini—Kṛṣṇa;
10. In Kaivalya—Śiva.

While discussing the delination of these characters we have kept in mind the historical development or variation in the depiction of these Chapters from the Ṛgveda to the Purāṇas.

Chapter IV—Philosophical Doctrines

In the dialogues are met with various descriptions of Brahman, the Brahmaloka, the sacred places etc., views regarding the metaphysical, eschatological, cosmological, psychological, ethical and moral problems, metempsychesis and life after death, incarnation etc. These topics are examined here from a critical point of view.

Chapter V—Commentators

In this Chapter the views of the following commentators viz. Śaṅkarācārya, Rāmānujācārya, Madhvācārya, Vallabhācārya, Nimbārkācārya on the relevant passages are critically examined.

The First Section (A) of this Chapter consists of the interpretations of the relevant Śrutis according to the five ācāryas and also other commentators, where the bhāṣya or the ṭīka of the great ācāryas is not available. It may be noted that the available commentaries on the relevant portion are consulted.

The Second Section (B) of the Chapter contains the study of the relevant passages and the BRS in comparison on the basis of commentaries of the ācāryas.

REFERENCES

1. Diwakar, R.R., "Stories and dialogues from the upaniṣads"; pub. Bharatiya Vidya Bhavan, Bombay.
2. Gajendragadkar, P.B., "The Ten Principal Upaniṣads", Bharatiya Vidya Bhavan, Bombay.

CHAPTER I

CONCEPT OF BOON

The idea of varadāna is met in with the Vedic and Purāṇic literature. The UPs relate a number of stories and dialogues. Some of them have a boon as its motif or a starting point for the development of a story and expounding philosophical doctrines. The motif is a theme or a centre of idea around which the whole story is revolved. Motifs are used frequently in folklores. Bhavabhūti in the Mālatī-Mādhava and Kālidāsa in the Śākuntala viz. Bakulamālā and ring respectively, used the technique of motif to develop the plot. Sometimes the motif remains the same in different stories, but some changes are seen in other aspects of motif. In UPs the motif of 'Vara' is used around which philosophical ideas are woven and speculations are drawn. Stith Thompson[1] describes motif thus "It is unusual central theme unaltered in different stories which draws and holds our attention that we call it a motif."

Now coming to the boon-based stories taken up in this study the Vara (o-dāna) motif appears as unchangeable and a very central bulk or cream of the story. As there are two interlocuters, one of them is a granter and the other is a grantee. The bestowal of some reward or gift by a granter to the grantee is a common factor in all such stories. If Vara (o-dāna), is dropped out from the story, the whole story ends or paralysed.

Moreover, this central theme of Vara (o-dāna) may be unusual so far the philosophical ideas are taken into account. e.g. the vivid picture of "Light : Ātman" presented by

Yājñavalkya to Janaka cannot be compared to normal gift of wealth or grants of sons, land etc. Yājñavalkya harmonises the illuminating elements like sun, moon, fire, Ātman in such a way that it remains unparalelled. Every thought of a seer is new and uncommon, so far as the philosophical ideas are concerned.

The philosophical speculations are put in such a practical way that a person is amazed at the Seer's deep vision, intuition in presentation. It makes a man introvert and reflective.

Poets like Kālidāsa, used the concept of 'Vara' in the Raghuvaṁśa[2] and in the Kumārasambhava[3]. The word Vara (boon) is derived from √vṛ is desire or to choose i.e. desire or choice which is asked to be fulfilled by god or by a superior person.

Generally the meaning, of the word 'vara' comes nearer to the word āśīrvāda. The verbal expression of a wish or will that good may befall on someone is a blessing—, an āśīrvāda.[4] Where as a boon is a request or the favour requested became a reality or a factual situation.[5] An āśīrvāda is also a state of good fortune that results from the power of a particular words. The efficacy of blessing rests on the belief in the special potency of inharent in a word or in the utterance of a deity, and direct or indirect as the case may be. The act of blessing implies certain gestures as for examples putting one's hand on the head of a person who is to be blessed.

If a superior person gives blessing to a man it becomes true. It is well-known that ancient seer's possessed such remarkable powers, on account of that power whatever they spoke the very speech become a reality. Bhavabhūti makes a statement following this very concept in "Uttara-rāma-caritam".[6]

There is a microscopic difference between 'vara' and āśīrvāda, no doubt both the vocables are closely related to some extent semantically but blessing is a mere expression of one's good wish towards someone who is going to be the object of it. "That particular blessing may or may not be realised; while vara is more permanent in character and surer of fulfillment."[7] A vara is realisable. When a man bows down to a ṛṣi or an aged man the ṛṣi immediately utters "may your desire be fulfilled". This particular utterance is nothing but a blessing. A seer wished something good to a man. That good fortune may come into reality or may not come; but when a properly qualified person expresses e.g. (1) May you get a vigourous son[8] these words of the vaikhanasa becomes a boon to Duṣyanta. (2) In the Raghuvaṁśa 'May you get a son'[9]. This particular wish of a Kautsa ṛṣi happened to be a boon to his king. It was certain that Duṣyanta and Raghu will have a son respectively. Thus the boon has certainty. Kālidāsa also distinguished between vara and āśīrvāda.[10] Āśīrvāda is a general statement. It does not refer to any specific issue, While a boon is a specific declaration which is bound to be true. A vara can be given by a deity or by an seer who has the power to bring about its fulfilment. e.g. Kaṇva was possessed of Sidhi, therefore his words were happened to prove to be true according to Gautami—"May you have a son, a universal Monarch"[11]. It is intended to last identically without change. There is no time element for the purpose of its fulfilment. After its aim is fulfilled it is exhausted. Once a boon exhausts away its purpose it has nothing to fulfil further. A boon implied protection or the protection is a corollary to choice.

When a boon is given there are two participants. One is a granter of the boon and the other is a grantee. It is a sort of communication. The granter of the boon is always on a higher level and achievement.

In the UPs we come across a granter who is either a god or a sage or an eminent Brahmin; or a King. On the other hand the grantee is on a lower level in comparison with that of a granter. Hierarchical distinction in terms of caste or class is not a factor with reference to one's being a granter or grantee. The choosing of the boon was not obligatory but the grantee had full liberty or freedom in choice. The Upaniṣ adic study of boon shows that a person with an earnest desire for something approaches an alaukikasadhu[12] and expresses his desire which is fulfilled.

In some cases the desire is fulfilled without expression. Similarly the desire is not fulfilled though it is expressed. In UPs 'vara' is not an extra-ordinary power but on account of a realisation of metaphysical knowledge the granter offers it to the receiver. He offers to him whatever is expected or desired by him. He never 'pours' more than what is wanted or desired. Sometimes a 'boon' includes the grace of God. It is also known as Anugraha.[13] Anugraha is Dhātuprasād.[14] (ŚU 3.20)

The genesis of the boon (Vara √vṛ) can be traced to the RV wherein the various verbal forms like vṛṇite, vṛṇate, vṛṇimahe, vṛṇiṣva, avṛṇidhvam etc. occur.

The forms like vṛṇimahe (9.66.18), vṛṇe (3.12.3); vṛṇate (1.141.6) avṛṇīta (1.117.13); vṛṇīte (1.67.1) denote the sense of request of asking for or selection. All of them are explained with सम् + √भज् by sāy.

(1) In 9.66.18 it implies 'request', e.g. A seer requests the god to help for defeating enemy etc.

(2) In 1.141.6 Hota requests Agni with offering of the oblations like a king.

(3) In 1.117.3 a seer asks to come and sit on, to the Aśvins.

(4) In 1.67.1 and 8.25.13; it implies protection. A seer asks for protection either of their wealth or themselves.

(5) In 3.12.3, amd 3.12.5 सम् + √भज् implies the sense of worship.

15—A— The verb vṛṇite in the said ṛe 1.67.1 is rendered as 'to protect' by (say)[1]; "choosing (velankar)[2]; 'demand' (oldenberg)[3]; desires (Max Muller)[4]; 'wohlmeinende' (Geldner)[5]. Skanda[6] and Mudgala agrees with Sāy. Veṅkata[7] does not comment. Griffith differs in translation.[8]

15—B—8.25.13 in the said ṛe, it is rendered 'protection' (sāy)[1] elect (Griffith)[2]; 'erbitten' (Geldner)[3]; Skanda and Mudgala do not comment; Veṅkata[4] follows sāy.

16—(i) 3.12.3 The said ṛe is rendered as 'request' (Sāy); 'choose' (Oldenberg)[2]; "erkure" (Geldner)[3]; Skanda and Mudgala[4] do not explain. Veṅkata does not give parafrasing word for vṛṇe. He keeps the word as it is.

(ii) 3.12.5, the ṛe is rendered 'worship' by (Sāy)[1]; 'choose' (oldenberg)[2]; Skanda and Mudgala[3] do not comment. Veṅkata[3] does not comment; he keeps the word as it is. erbitte (Geldner)[4].

17—The verbal forms like Vṛṇīta 5.50.1; Vṛṇīmahe 10.36.2.7 implies the meaning as "favour", grace.

(i) 5.50.1 the said re is rendered as 'favour' (Sāy)[1]; "freundchaft" (Geldner)[2]; expect, prosper (Veṅkata)[3]; Mudgala agrees with Sāy.

(ii) 10.36.2-7—It is rendered as "prosper, favour" by (Sāy)[1]; 'grace' (Griffith)[2]; "erbitten" (Geldner)[3]; Udgītha and Veṅkata agrees with sāy.[4]

18—(i) In 10.91.8-9; 5.20.3; 10.33.4, the verbal forms implies the meaning of choice or selection to illustrate in the 10.91.8-9, the verbal form Vṛnate is rendered as 'select' (Sāy)[1]; 'select' (Griffith).[2]

(ii) In 10.164.2 vṛṇate implies the sense of praying, or invoking. The said ṛc is rendered as 'pray' by (Sāy)[1], 'elect' (Griffith)[2]; 'wahl' (Geldner)[3]; Skanda and Mudgala do not comment. Veṅkata keeps the word as it is'.

(iii) In 6.17.8, vṛṇate occurs, in the sense of 'invocation'; it is rendered as 'invoking' by (Say)[1]; "chose" (Griffith)[2]; "erwahlen" (Geldner)[3].

(iv) In the ṛc 10.13.4 the verbal form avṛnīta implies "praying". It is rendered as 'pray' by (Sāy)[1], 'chose' (Griffith)[2]; Zog (Geldner)[3]; Udgitha[4] agrees with sāy. elect, choose, (Velankar)[5]; "erwahlen" (Geldner)[6].

(v) 5.20.3 vṛṇīmahe it is rendered as 'choose' (Say)[1]; choose (Griffith)[2]; erwahlt (Geldner)[3]. Veṅkata and Mudgala[4] agree with Sāy.

(vi) 10.33.4. Avṛni—it is rendered as 'select' by (Sāy)[1]; 'choose' (Griffith)[2]; "erwahlt" (Geldner)[3]; "Pray" (Udgitha, Veṅkaṭa)[4]; Skanda[5] do not comment.

19—(i) The nominal form vara occurs as vára and vará. In ṛc 1.119.3. It is rendered as 'highest' (Sāy)[1]; 'choice boon' (Griffith)[2] "Wunsch" (Geldner)[3]; śreṣ ṭha (skanda)[4]; 'highest'[5] (Mudgala and Veṅkaṭa).[5]

(ii) In 1.140.13, the verbal form varanta is rendered as 'obtained' (Sāy)[1] 'choose' (Griffith)[2]; 'Lohngabe'

(Geldner)[3]; "choose" (Velankar)[4]; choose (Oldenberg)[5]; "choose" (Veṅkata)[6].

Thus it is clear that the √vṛ is interpreted as having the following nuances. It can be concluded that 'vara' has the sense of praying, choosing asking for etc. The word vara occurs in the RV with ādyudātta and antodātta i.e. Vára (choice, selection, a action noun) and vara (agent noun).[20] The seer expects protection, friendship; rewards like heroic sons, wealth, cattles, horses which would be helpful to them. In the 10th Maṇḍala only, ṛṣi is seen to be praying for removing darkness from the heart. In the 1.12 it is mentioned that they wanted wealth and food which would produce heroic, vigourous sons.

In the environment of the verbal or nominal forms of √vṛ we do not have situations where somebody is made to be please by somebody for somebody. The ṛṣi himself chooses generally something for himself. In RV we do not find a situation parallel the situation to UP(s) i.e. X chooses Y object but there is no A to tell X to choose in Saṁhitā.

AV—In the AV 'vara' is connected with the sense of the highest fruit. The forms of √vṛ or vara occur rarely in AV.

The nominal form varāya[22] in 16.6.10 is rendered as 'highest fruit by (sāy)[1]; highest fruit of deeds (Satavalekar)[2].

In 20.77.6 the verbal form means desired object.

The nominal form varāya[23] in 7.3.1 is rendered as for the highest fruit (sāy)[1]; by (Whitney)[2].

The verbal form vṛṇe[24] in 7.15.1; is rendered by as to beg (sāy)[1]; 'to accept' by (Sātavalekar)[2].

YV—In YV the √vṛ means also to choose to obtain. The YV gives the following stories which enables us to get a picture of the concept 'vara'—

I. Prajāpati created offsprings, they being created went away from him and they went to Varuṇa. He pursued them and asked them to be returned but Varuṇa disagreed with Prajāpati and then he said, "choose a boon and give them to me". Prajāpati prays to Varuṇa by saying that in this creation that which is the highest (vara) take it and remaining part give back to him (Prajāpati). Varuṇa touched to the black beast with one white foot—saying—"this is mine". (2.1.2.1)

II. When Indra requested earth to share a third part of his guilt at the time of killing of Viśvā vapu—domestic priest of gods; the earth put a condition "Let me choose a boon". By that boon she wished not to overcome through digging. (2.5.1.2)

III. In 2.5.2.57 dyāvā Pṛthivī wished to have to be adorned with Nakṣatrās with variegated things by Indra, in the battle of Vṛtra.

IV. When Agni departed from gods, gods requested to come back to them for carrying out the oblations. Herein Agni put a condition by chosing the boon in the form of offering Vājaprasavīya in the sacrifice. 5.4.9.1.

V. Similarly Aditi, the goddess, is seen to fulfil her desire that she wanted opening and concluding oblations in the sacrifice; when the gods were uncertain in fixing the quarters on the vedi. They requested Aditi to help in distinguishing quarters. (6.1.5.1.)

VI. Rudra also put a condition by choosing a boon—that he will be a overlord of animals. In the afore going stories the following points may be concluded. The expression of the words varam vṛṇiṣva; varam vṛnai; expect either a share in sacrifice; superiority over the animals; a share of cup in rites etc. That means in YV the boon is offered on the lower level. Moreover it becomes a condition for other. A person gets something in exchange of otherthing. (6.2.3.2).

In this narration the boon is indirect and conditional. The boon becomes a condition for giving the creation to Prājāpati for example 2.1.21.

In YV the boon has barter at its base, and not in the UPs. In YV there is a semantic development of √vṛ. Brahmā Brahmā created, Varuṇa takes away Brahmā's Creation. tells Varuṇa—"choose a boon" that is offering of boon is clear (Y); but the boon is not specified.

Prajāpati (A) tells Varuṇa (x)—"Give them to me". Varuṇa's choice is not known. Prajāpati orders for the choice and Varuṇa has to return to Brahmā his creation. Thus one thing is missing in this story.

Brāhmaṇas—

In Brāhmaṇas, some more light is thrown on the problem of vara. The AB informs about different sacrificial rites; in which some short stories are referred in the context of the gods granting the boons to the other gods for example 1.2.1.[25]

The stories are as follows—

I The Aditi goddess asked for a boon, when the presiding deities over the sacrifice went away from gods because of some reason; those gods felt that they were unable to perform any rite in connection with the sacrifice. So the gods went to Aditi and asked for her favour by which they would come to know the Yajñakarma. Moreover they would be active enough to do those sacrificial acts. Aditi's boon refers to the sacrificial rite, viz—In the soma-yaga, rice would be offered to Aditi in the opening and concluding rites and as per her wish the eastern direction would be known after her.[27]

II. Mitrāvaruṇa obtained a boon from the gods e.g. offering of Payasyā[28] in the morning pressing of the Soma sacrifice when gods asked them for removing faults in the morning pressing ceremony. 2.3.12.

III. Another story is referred in which Rudra chooses a boon from gods when they came to know that Prajāpati is acting sinfully. It was a censurable act on the part of Prajāpati. Gods requested Rudra to shoot Prajāpati with his arrow as Rudra is considered having giant and terrific form. He agreed to gods, requested if the vara that he would have command over animals is approved of hence his epithet Paśupati. 3.9.

Thus according to the AB the boon is granted by laying down a condition to a granter. It is not mere a giving and a taking; but the giver of the boon asks some kind of work to be done by the receiver, and then the receiver agrees to the giver in exchange according to the wish. The boons in the AB are associated with the sacrificial acts and not to epistomology as in Ups. The recipient of the boon does not ask for wealth, cattle, land etc. as the Saṁhitās. On the contrary they are in the need of having a share in the sacrificial rites. They are satisfied with the offerings of the oblations. AB narrates a boon as a reward / payment. e.g. It is done in response to the service done.

SB

SB 4.1.1.21; 3.1.4.18 and 19; 1.1.3.84; 6.1.19 uses the √vṛ in the sense of "to choose" to illustrate.

SB—3.2.5.4; 1.1.3849.

Indra chose waters for their help while fighting with Vṛtra.

In the TA verbal form vṛṇase occurs in the sense of praying for example : 6.4.2 the dead body is free to go where pitṛs are prayed for; and it goes with Pitṛs to the highest place also with the performance of Iṣṭāpurta karma.

2. The verbal form vṛṇati means pervading in 3.11.3.
3. In 2.2.1 Prajāpati offers a boon to who practises hard penance. Having been pleased with them he gave a boon that Āditya will be their leader. Prajāpati permitted to fight with Āditya. Herein the reason for granting a boon is mentioned i.e. performance of penance.

The KS[29] mentions directly that the boon is Ātman; Ātman is the highest element. Thus the nominal and verbal forms of the √vṛ are commonly used in the vedic literature √vṛ = to choose when Agni is chosen as a messenger. RV does not give parallel cases as those of Ups.

The AV and the Yv reflect those objects connected with the sacrificial rites, sacrificial objects. The Yv has short stories introduced in between the directions of a ritual. This reminds us about the comment with reference to Brāhmaṇas viz. "legends are like oasis in the desert."[30] There is no hierarchy between the granter and the recipient of the boon in the Yv. The Brāhmaṇas are the connecting link between the vedic and the upaniṣadic literature. They are helpful for the understanding of the later philosophical literature. The stories in the Brāhmaṇas give mostly, the directions for the performance of the sacrificial rites and ceremonies, and the sacrificial gifts. Although the stories concern with the creation, or the cosmogonic element, or the sociology or the other sciences like Geometry, astronomy, etc.; all of them have the sacrificial motive at their base. "Tremendous importance is ascribed to the sacrifice."[31] It may be observed that the sacrifice is the ruling principle over all. It is the highest aim of the life. It is a power which governs the nature. Thus the sacrifice is ranked at a high grade at that period. All the stories have the sacrifice as their background around which all the discussions start; on which everything depends. And this ritualism is changed into the philosophy later on in the Upaniṣadic time.

Now coming to the Ups, we are able to gather more information, and form some clear and concrete picture about the nature, contents and the participants of the boon. We find that the contents of a boon refer to metaphysical knowledge. The granter possesses knowledge with mastery in a particular branch of knowledge. The recipient does not have an extra-ordinary siddhi, but he is inquisitive to know about further movement of jīva when it passes away; and by which path does it proceed and the place where it reaches ! This means that boons are related to eschatology and metempsychosis. The granter or receiver of the boon never puts a condition reciprocally; when a boon is asked for, and granted. It becomes essential to fulfil the contents of the boon asked for on the part of the granter. The recipient never asked for material wealth but was eager to have progress in spiritual path. At the time of vara (o-dāna) the receiver of the boon selects the granter, he approaches to a granter and asks to fulfil his desired object. The experts were known to them and therefore they approach to them. The person who approaches, tries to please the person approached; by some or other way that may be a modest behaviour; or mature in a mind and intellect. The aspirants are not isolent or attacking; they do not revolt while they try to please him with a pleasing manners. There after the granter examines that person approached and observes him, if he is entitled to secure or not entitled to secure that secret knowledge. The granter gives to the point knowledge, and does not speak about more than wanted.

In the epic Rāmāyaṇa the boons and curses go together. The boon to one becomes curse to the other viz. when the king Daśaratha offered a boon to the queen Kaikeyi i.e. "the consecration of her son as the heir for the kingdom," becomes a curse on the part of Rāma and Rāma's mother.

The boons and the curses function significantly in the life of the Rāma, the son of the king Daśaratha. The number of crisises in the life of Rāma like the Rāma's exile in the forest fot the 14 years; the abduction of the Sītā; etc. are due to the boons and curses.[32] The king Daśaratha's promise to the Kaikeyi is a curse indisguise of a boon. The boons in the Rāmāyaṇa lead to the development of the plot. The story does not lead to the exposition of the philosophy as compared to those stories of the Ups.

Sometimes the boon becomes remedy over a curse[33] viz. in the legend of the Garuḍa, the wife of the Kaśyapa was cursed by her son viz. Aruṇa, because of her hasty nature. He gave a curse that she would have been a slave to her co-wife (Kadrū) for five hundred years further. It is told that she would be made free from the slavery by her (Vinatā) second son. Thus Aruṇa's speech is a curse which would be turned into a boon.

Some stories in the MbH.[34] does not proceed further. They remain static in a way, viz. Indra and Agni granted a boon to the Śibi when they were pleased with the king. The gods bestowed upon him the everlasting fame. The story does not develop the plot or it does not expound the philosophical doctrine, as the stories compared to those in the Rāmāyaṇa and the Ups. respectively.

In the Vana Parvan[35] of the MbH, the story of the Sāvitrī, the daughter of the king Aśvapati, is narrated. Sāvitrī obtained five boons when Yama, was pleased with her. The story is narrated as follow. Sāvitrī knew the time of death of her husband i.e. Satyavāna; from the Nārada before her marriage with the Satyavāna. She observed the vow of "Trirātra" and she followed her husband intentionally when Satyavāna started to go to the forest. In the evening Satyavāna did not feel well and so he went to sleep. At that time Yama, the god of death came to take out the life of Satyavāna. Sāvitrī followed Yama when he carried out the life of Satyavāna. Yama requested her to go back again and again but with her wise and intellectual talk, she hold conversation with Yama and pleased him. Yama asked to choose a boon except the life of her husband. Sāvitrī obtained the boons viz. 1. Restoration of the eye-sight of her father-in-law 2. Achievement of the kingdom for her father-in-law 3. Hundred sons to her father viz. Aśvapati 4. Hundred sons in the race of Satyavāna having united with her husband 5. The life of Satyavāna.

It may be observed from the above mentioned story that the story lays down the vow for the achievement of the desired object. The physical form of the granter is also described where as in the Ups the bodily description, of the granter is not found. In the Sāvitrī upākhyāna, Yama's dreadful form is described as having a large body of a darkish colour; red eyes, a noose in the hand. He is compared with the Sun in effulgency. Yama appeared like a cald in red attire with the head decked with a diadem.

The story mentions the reason of pleasing by a granter to the grantee viz. the pious and ascetic merits and her wise and reasonable talk.

In this story the grantee is not free to ask for the desired object bur the granter put the condition to the grantee. Thus the boon becomes conditional though it differs from those of the Brāhmaṇas. In the Brāhmaṇas when the boon is offered; some kind of work is expected to be done for the other. While in this story of the MbH, Yama did not expect any kind of work or object in the exchange from the grantee. Yama showed his readiness to fulfil Sāvitrī's desired object, except the life of her husband. At the beginning Sāvitrī asked for boons which were chosen for the good of the others and not for herself—she asked for the material happiness. Thus the boons chosen by Sāvitrī fall in the group of mānu-Ṣa-vitta. They do not lead to the spiritual happiness. Yama granted her with more than wanted He (gave) granted the great fame and success in the world, to the Satyavāna. He also gave four hundred years life to the Satyavāna with his sons and the grand sons, while in the Upaniṣadic stories the granter of the boon grants the object which is asked for. Thus this type of development is seen in the Epic and it is developed in the Purāṇas.

II. Arjuna acquired the weapon from Śiva when Śiva was pleased with Arjuna due to his severe penance.[36] In this story the command of Yudhishthira made Arjuna to go to the Kāmyakavana for obtaining the sight of Śiva. The story refers to the performance of the hard penance as the necessary cause for getting the desired object. The Arjuna performed hard penance viz. He used to eat the leaves fallen upon the ground from the trees and some fruits, after the interval of the six nights and then at the interval of the fortnight. After the month he stopped eating of the leaves and the fruits. The Arjuna performed the auesterity with the arms upraised leaning upon nothing and stood on the tips of his toes. The story refers to the type of auesterity for the achievement of the boon. Then after the effect of the Arjuna's penance is mentioned viz. the earth smoked all around due to his asceticism.

The Śiva appeared in the form of a Kirāta and fought with the Arjuna severally. A fierceful combat between the Arjuna and Kirāta is described in the story. Śiva leaved the Kirāta's form and revealed himself. The Śiva praised Arjuna and granted him an irresistible weapon and also the immortal eyes to see the form of the Śiva, The Śiva told the reason of pleasing viz. the Arjuna was unequal in the courage and the patience. Strength and the prowess among the Kṣatriyas. Thus the reason of pleasing with the grantee is told by the granter.

The Arjuna praised the Śiva viz. the granter, with bending down on his knee and bowed with his head. Thus the posture of the grantee is pointed out when the grantee worshipped the granter. The physical form of the granter is also described. viz. the Śiva, having blue throat matted lock. The Śiva is addressed as the chief of the gods, the refuge of all the gods. The ruling principle etc. The Arjuna asked for the Śiva's protection and asked to forgive him because he had not recognised the Śiva when he fought with the Kirāta. The Śiva informed about the past life of the Arjuna. This is a peculiar development in the boon's nature found in the MbH. In the Saṁhitās, the Brāhmaṇas or in the Ups. Such type of description is not found.

The Arjuna wished to have such a weapon from the lord Śiva which would be destroyed at the end of Yuga, the entire universe. By that terrible weapon Arjuna would obtained the victory in the terrible conflict between the Pāṇḍavas and the Kauravas. The weapon which when hurled with the mantras should produce the thousands of darts; and the fiercelooking maces and arrows like the snakes of verulent poison. The lord Śiva offered, him his favourite weapon viz. the 'Paśupata' with the knowledge of hurling and withdrawing it. The god Śiva put a condition to Arjuna about the use of the Weapon viz.—The weapon should not be hurled without adequate cause if it hurled at any enemy if little might in may destroy the whole universe.

Further Purāṇas also refer to a number of boons. The VP. has the vocable vara in sense of choosing, selecting.

I. The VP (300-500 A.D.)[37] mentions a boon by Parāśara to Pulastya that he would be a narrator of the Purāṇas. Apparently the boon does not seem to be dealing with very deep concept of philosophy. The philosophy which it discusses from the dialogue between Maitreya and Parāśara is somewhat similar to that of vedas and that of Ups.

   viz. Cosmology, physics etc. Here the highest entity is Viṣṇu and not the Brahman. Viṣṇu is connected with the ruling of the universe. He is all pervading, eternal, imperishable and also the root cause of creation. The VP answers to the questions with reference to the cosmos. (VP I.1.)

II. Dhruva, the son of Uttānapāda attains immutable position through the worship of Viṣṇu. The legend is narrated as follows : He was insulted by his step mother viz. Suruchi so he cherished the desire to obtain such place that it shall be honoured universally. Dhruva, a small child wished to get such a station as none before him has attained. Dhruva's desired object was not related to the worldly objects like dominion, or all kinds of riches and royal pleasures being a king's child; but it was beyond the reach of man and which was difficult to be obtained. Dhruva performed a hard penance immensed his mind in deep contemplation and so Viṣṇu was pleased with him. (VP 99 adhyāya ft.) He asked him a desired object Viṣṇu tells him the reason of pleasing to him.

Unlike Ups the VP presents a full bodily description of a granter i.e. Viṣṇu—bearing a Conch, a discuss, a mace and a bow in his hand Dhruva praises Viṣṇu, on the contrary Upaniṣadic recipient does not praise. Viṣṇu bestows the station, above the three worlds at the end. These are Purāṇic developments.

III. The story of Mārīśā is related to Maitreya by Parāśara in which she prays to Viṣṇu to grant husbands in succeeding births and also a son equal to a Patriarch amongst men. Moreover she also wished to be possessed of affluence and beauty. (1.15-61ff.)

IV. Diti's son Hiraṇyakaśipu obtained power over all the three worlds. (1.20.21).

V. Prahlāda, the son of Hiraṇyakaśipu had an unflinching faith in Viṣṇu and he devoted himself constantly to him in succeeding births. Further Prahlāda requested the god to forgive his father for various sins. Viṣṇu granted his request. The story mentions one more boon though it was not asked for viz. Prahlāda will attain freedom from existence due to Viṣṇu's grace. (VP. 1.17).

VI. Sagar gets a boon that his grandson would bring down the Ganges on the earth. (VP. 4.4.12).

VII. Pururavas asked the Gandharvas for the lifelong company of Urvaśī (8 FF).

I. In the MP (260 A.D. to 400 A.D.)[38] Diti, the mother of demons practised penance and obtained the Cāndrāyaṇa vrata to please the ṛṣis. She asked for a vrata that would free her from the crushing grief of her son's distruction and make her happy in this world as well as in the other world. The sage Vasiṣṭha advised her to observe the Madana-dvādaśī vrata by observing which Diti become the mother of Maruts and was liberated from the pangs of grief. The sage describes Madana-dvādaśī vrata. (MP. 7.7.)

II. Pīvarī, the daughter of Barhiṣad Pitṛs practised severe penance for a long time. Viṣṇu was pleased with her devotion and appeared before her. She prayed for a beautiful husband; Yogic powers, and would be able to curb her passions. The Lord granted more than expected. viz. blessed her with a daughter who was to be well versed in Yoga to be the mother of Kṛṣṇa, Gaura and Śambha who will be great mahatmans and also attain herself mokṣa after having given birth to such illustrious sons. MP 15.7.4)

Actually the attainment of mokṣa was not asked for but Viṣṇu "Pours" more than receiver's wish. Pīvarī asked for a manly husband that is a kind of mānuṣavitta, while mokṣa can be placed on a higher level than material rewards. Further the MP mentions the future of next generations who would have remarkable acquired merits.

III. Anagha—the son of Vibhrāja also seeked to have powerful, illustrious dutiful son who would be well-versed in all Śāstras and Yoga; well conversant with the languages of all the creatures. This boon comes under the mānuṣavitta. (MP 21 ff.)

IV. In the Śukrācāryākhyāna, the method of tapas is stated. Śukra, observed that method, viz. a vow of smoke i.e. the penance with suspended down head; imbibing the smoke of chaft for a thousand years. Śukra praises Viṣṇu similar to that of Dhruva praised in the VP (MP 47 ff)

V. In the legend of Prahlāda, Prahlāda succeeded in obtaining the boon from Śukra, after Śukra had cursed them that asuras would loose their intellect and would be defeated by the Devas. At that time Prahlāda stood before him in repentence along with Asuras with their heads cast down in shame. Śukra moved with pity and compassion, so granted a boon to remove the effect of his curse. Boon becomes remedy over a curse in this story. (MP 47 ff.) Śukra told that Asuras would obtain wealth in future. The curse would be effective. It can not be changed because fate is stronger. That means the effect of a curse was certain but not permanent. In the story of a boon. The element of fate is brought in. That means a boon is related to fate. It is more powerful than boon according to the MP. Herein daiva philosophy is operating. viz. Fate is everything in man's life.[39]

VI. Brahmā granted boons to Daityas viz. Maya and Tārakāsura. Maya wanted to build a fort which would be free from the attacks of enemies, and impregnable and if not possible it was to be vulnerable by one arrow only shot once by Śiva in the course of the battle. Tārakāsura demon wanted to overcome death and consequently he practised penance to please him who remarked to him that no living being could escape from the rewards of Karma, and therefore in his haughtiness he asked for his death at the hands of a babe of seven days old. (MP 129 ff.)

This story has a reference to the philosophy of Karma and it does not refer to the problem of mokṣa and the Vara-Prāpti gives temporary exemption from the rewards of the action.

VII. The demon Hiraṇyakaśipu practised hard penance for 11000 years. He took his bath regularly and then plunged himself in neck-deep water and observed the vow of silence. He also restrained and controlled his passions. The MP stresses that there is no greater ascetic than one who strictly follows celibacy by subjugating all his passions. (MP—161 ff.)

The reason of performing tapas is stated when in the Harikeśākhyāna the father orders Hari Keśa to go and practice penance in Kāśi.

I. The BHP (5th century A.D. to the 10th century)[40] mentions the specific form of a granter of the boon viz. Viṣṇu.* Similarly the BHP emphasised on the prescribed modes of worship and deep meditation as necessary for tapas in the story of Kardama. Viṣṇu is pleased with him and appeared before him in the form of Brahmā, having lotus feet seated on Garuḍa bright as the Sun with a garland of white lotus and blue water lily; adorned with a crown and ear-pendants a conchshell in his hand, the mace, Śrivatsa mark on his breast, Kaustubha jewel hung on his neck; Kardama fell at the feet of the Lord when He appeared before him and praised him. Kardama wanted to marry with a girl of similar disposition who would bring all the best that one wishes as a householder. Viṣṇu bestowed on his desired object and also said "you will attain Me; you with your controlled senses will see yourself and the world as identical with me and Me with yourself." The speech of Viṣṇu is advaitic. (BHP 21 adhyaya ff.)

II. Viṣṇu blessed Pṛthu. He told the king that the

attainment of his favour was not easy. It is not easily obtained by the practice of penance, or by Yoga, or by Sacrificial acts. The Lord abides in the 'hearts of those who have equipoised state. It also stressed that if a man worships the Lord constantly, faithfully disinterestedly by performing his duties prescribed by scriptures. The devotee's mind becomes pure gradually. When the mind becomes pure, the sense-pleasures do not attract a man and then only a man finds peace, oneness with Brahmā. The mental and physical state of Pṛthu is noticable in this story i.e. when the Lord is pleased, the king stood with folded hands, before Him. He could not look at him because of His lustre, the King's eyes were full of tears, the throat was choked up by tears and he was unable to speak. He asked for ten thousands ears. The Lord's voice was a supra thing in relation to yogic powers, wealth, sons and even liberation. Through it he liked to keep Lord's memory live in his heart. (BHP. 4.20)

III. The story of Prācetas also shows that Lord appears in a form compact of pure sattva dispelling their weariness. His radiant lustre looked like a cloud on a peak of Meru.

The intention of the father's order is that prācetas should carry out penance by plunging into the waters of ocean and by propitiating Hari, by japa. They also regard the attachment with the Lord is the best thing. The Lord bestowed on them every kind of wealth. (BHP 4.30 ff.)

IV. Hiraṇyakaśipu wanted to make himself invincible, immortal remain young, become the sole unrivaled ruler of the earth. He therefore went to the mandāra mountain to practise an extra-ordinary penance. The story describes another way of tapas viz. standing on toes with the arms stretched upwards, eyes fixed on the sky. The effect of tapas on devotee's body is that a fire mixed with smoke broke out of his head, spread over all sides and it heated the worlds above, below and all around the earth. Gods requested Brahmā to put an end of this severe tapas; so Brahmā, the giver of boon came there and asked him his desire. Then Brahmā sprinkled holy water from his gourd[41] on the Daitya's body. This water was drunk up by the ants and other insects. Then Hiraṇyakaśipu came out of that hill of earth and grass; looked like gold, strong and brave. Brahmā transmutes his form. This an example of getting immortal form when the granter of the boon is pleased. In the Upaniṣadic boon-based stories the receiver's form is not transmuted. (BHP 7.3-5)

V. Once Bali worshipped the Lord by the performance of the horse-sacrifice. When the Lord was pleased, entered the sacrificial place in the form of Vāmana. Bali offered a promise to fulfil his desire. The Brahmin asked for a little piece of land, just three placesin length, measured by his feet. Bali gave him the land according to his promise; by pouring water into his hand. (BHP 8.20) The period for tapas also increases. Purāṇa give thousand years period for a penance. This is in accordance with its usual style. The story of Hiraṇyakaśipu mentions one lakhs years of practising of penance.

VAP (between 350 - 550 A.D.)[42] denotes the vocable 'vara' in two meanings 1. highest, of best; Superior. 2. Boon. In 33.14 and 52.98 the vocable 'vara' means highest i.e.

Dhruva is highest than Agni, Kaśyapa. In 55.60, VAP emphasises constant faith on god, as superior to all. The Yogins are asked to have faith on Śiva, when Śiva was pleased.

In 32.53 in the course of the narration there is a reference to 'vara' viz. boon it states that the kings from Yayāti generation obtained long-life, wealth fame and prosperity in the form of eight siddhis.

The narrative describes Śiva's form as that in the BHP i.e. Śiva putting on flowers and sandal paste on the body, holding the bow in his hand namely Pināka; riding on the bull, staff and trident (triśūla) in his hand; fierceful etc.

Śiva obtained a boon from Brahmā that Pitṛs have a share in Śrāddha-ritual. Men may worship Pitṛs with sandal paste, flowers, rice-balls, first to pitṛs and then to the gods. (5.16)

Sagara obtained rewards from Kapilamuni e.g. the reward of performance of hundred aśvamedha sacrifices; the constant dwelling in the heaven and a vigourous son called Samudra. (26.148)

VAP 30.42 describes rewards like long-life, gold, son thousand hands etc.

VAP narrates the rewards obtained which may be called as material objects (Preyas) and not śreyas. There is no communication of two participants as in Ups. or other Purāṇas like VP, BHP, MP etc. some of the narrations refer to the usual practices and common beliefs among men.

The BRP (between 4th and 6th century A.D.)[43] also narrates the boons obtained by various persons; when it is used adjectively, 'vara' (of Varau) means highest and it does not refer to any highest principle or Lord; but it refers to ṛṣi[44] (BHP 1.11.2)

II. Śiva grants the grantee that the latter would have

constant devotion / faith steadfast in him by the varadāna. (BRP 1.2.26-29).

III. Indra grants a boon to the ṛṣi that he would obtain incomparable vigourous disciples well versed in all saṁhitās. (BRP 1.2.35.32)

IV. The daughter of Puloma got a boon that she would obtain a son who would be divine and supreme among brahmavits. (BRP 23.55.40)

V. Aṁśumān, the son of Sagar asked "if you grant me a boon, all my pitṛs will get immutable Brahman, and eternal place and your anger would be pacified. On account of your favour they will secure heaven (BRP 3.4.12.3-7)

The examples of boons in the BRP consider heaven as covetable place possibly according to them there is no higher place than heaven.

VI. The same thought occurs in the boon granted by Śiva to Triśaṅku : that he would get heaven with his bodily form.

VII. Śiva offers a boon to the child of Gauri and gives missiles and weapons. (BRP 3.4.12.3-7)

VIII. The goddess Lalita declared that whatsoever worshipped her with devotion would always get Śrī, Yaśas, and dharma and they would be free from any danger anbd that they would be happy and that they would obtain vidyā, vinaya and long-life. (BRP 3.4.13.30)

The BRP mentions the granting of the boons either to the gods or to munis or to ṛṣis. In it the boons are not granted through dialogues while the BRP relates the stories in brief or it narrates the boon. The requisites like sincere faith, devotion play an important role in the attainment of a desired fruit; and not mānuṣa-vitta. From the afore going Purāṇic boon-based stories, the concept of vara regarding its contents, nature and style emerges as follows :—

The VP discusses the problems of the creation, dissolution etc. wherein it accepts Viṣṇu as underlying principle of the universe and it gives the Sāṁkhyan cosmogonical account wherein the Puruṣa is created from Viṣṇu and then other elements like Pradhāna, Prakṛti, Kāla etc. are evolved.

In the VP is told the Dhruvākhyāna. Where in Dhruva's choice is related to daiva-vitta and not mānuṣa-vitta. e.g. a station, none before him has attained Daiva-vitta implies knowledge with reference to Ups. The term daiva-vitta can be extended to Purāṇas. It may be included the heaven which is regarded supreme place. The VP emphasises on contemplation and penance for the fulfilment of the desired object while in Ups penance is not an essential requirement in all cases.

The granter of a boon in the Purāṇas tells the reason of being pleased. e.g. indifference towards worldly objects and constant thinking of Him alone by Dhruva; whereas in Ups while a boon is being offered, the reason of being pleased, are not expressed directly. Some currents of hints thereto or indirect suggestions on are found in the Saṃhitās, Brāhmaṇas and Ups. The Purāṇas develop the ideas further which are latent in Ups.

The Purāṇas present a full bodily description of a granter e.g. In the VP, Viṣṇu is described as having a Conch, a discus a mace, a bow in his hand. The BHP elaborates the specific form of a granter of the boon. The grantee praises the granter of the boon. Almost all the stories mention more objects which are not asked for or wished by a grantee. Sometimes mokṣa is not asked for but the god frees the devotee from his Karmic bondage through his grace. The boon does not give mokṣa as its reward; it gives temporary exemption from the rewards of action. The tapas certainly bears a reward, but that the reward has some limit. Sometimes the Purāṇas do not mention imperishable rewards like mukti as Ups do. Sometimes this has an advaitic tone. The VP refers to both the kinds of boons viz. Śreyas and Preyas. They add new ideas which are not found in the early vedic literature. The Purāṇas refer to devotion, contemplation, sincere faith as means to boons as Ups do. BHP stresses the prescribed modes of worship, as well as meditation as requisite for tapas. Sometomes the method of penance is described and the reasons for tapas are also given e.g. The penance with a head suspended down and imbing the smoke of chaft for a thousand years. Continuously restraining and controlling passions. The MP directly expresses that there is no greater ascetic than one who strictly follows celibacy by subjugating all his passions.

The Purāṇic boons are offered on the basis of supernatural powers. They do not deal with the metaphysical knowledge only, but the concept of boon changes here. It is connected with extra-ordinary divine favour. A person is sure to obtain any difficult object, with the god's grace.

Sometimes Purāṇas lay down rituals and vows for the accomplishment of one's desire. Sometimes the benevolent effect of the vara takes on the succeeding generations with the total satisfaction of the recipient of the vara. One more development about the nature of boon can be pointed out viz. a boon becomes a remedy for a curse after its expirary. In this connection, sometimes, there is a role of daiva (fate) in the operation of the boon.

Sometimes a boon is obtained for the sake of others rather than for one's own's self. Sometimes the area of operation of a boon expands e.g. in the case of Sāvitri.

It also refers to the Upaniṣadic thought that the attainment of a god's grace is not easy. The god can not be obtained by the practice of penance; yoga, or by sacrificial acts. The God 'reveals' himself to the devotee.[46] Sometimes in such description there is a philosophical description also. The Lord's grace comes to be known as supreme one. The devotee asks fot the voice of a Lord by which he would like to keep Lord's memory fresh in the heart. All other things like Yogic powers, wealth, sons, even liberation from life are unimportant, or unconsiderable to a devotee. It is neither Karma, nor knowledge, nor devotion alone; but the Lord's grace is enough powerful to make a many happy devoice of all wories.

Moreover the physical state of a grantee is noticeable in some stories while Ups do not refer to it. Another important point may be referred to in connection with the concept of the boon, viz. the grantee's form may change or assume a new form. The descriptions of gods enable us to help in iconic worship which is still to be continued.

In BHP the boons are granted either to a god or to a muni or to a ṛṣi. It seems that both participants are of equal grade e.g. gods. When a boon is being offered, one god approaches another god. The approaching god wants some help or reward from the approached god. Thus the approached god is higher than the approaching god.Thus the hierarchy is created for the time being and the phenomenon of heirarcy between the two interlocuters remains same throughout.

REFERENCES

1. Thompson Stith quoted by Arora Udai Prakash, "Motif in Indian Mythology", Introduction, p. 14.
2. Kālidāsa, Raghuvaṁśa 2.63.
   "Prītāsmi te putra varaṁ vṛṇiṣva".
3. Kālidāsa, Kumārasaṁbhava 2.32.
   "bhavallabdha varodīrṇaḥ".

4. On boon and blessing vide Encyclopaedia of Britannica, Vol. III.
5. On boon and blessing vide Encyclopaedia of Britannica, Vol. III.
6. Bhavabhūti, Uttara-rāma-caritam, 1.10.
"ṛṣiṇām punarādyānām vāconurthonudhāvati."
7. Gode P.K. and Karve C.G. (ed.) Principal Vaman Shivaram Apte, The Practical Sanskrit-English Dictionary, Part III, p. 1390.
8. Kālidāsa, Abhijñāna Śākuntala, Act. I, p. 8.
"chakravartin putram avāpnuhi"
9. Kālidāsa, Raghuvaṁśa, 5.34.
10. Kālidāsa, Abhijñāna Śākuntala, Act. IV, p. 102.
11. Kālidāsa, Abhijñāna Śākuntala, 4.7, p. 101.
12. A term used by R.D. Karmarkar, Abhijñāna Śākuntala, Notes, p. 290.
13. "poṣaṇam tadanugrah" BHP. 2.10.1.
14. Śu. 3.20. Ś. Comm. धानुरीश्वरस्य प्रसादात्। प्रसन्ने हि परमेश्वरे तद्याथात्म्यज्ञान-मुत्पद्यते; अथवा इंद्रियाणि धातवः शरीरस्य धारणातेषां प्रसादाविषयदोष दर्शनमारुध-पनयनात्।।
vide. Radhakrishnan, S., The Principle Upaniṣads, p. 730. dhātu-prasādāt—"sense organs are said to be dhātu". Ś reads dhātuḥ = Iśvarsya as mentioned.
15. —A 1. Sāy. Com. 1.67.1.
एवं भूतं यजमानं वृणीते संभजते। अनेन प्रतं हविः स्वीकृत्य रक्षतीतिभावः।।
   2. JUB, Vol. XXXI (New series) Sept. 1962; p. II; p. 5. Agni hymns 1-2.
   3. Oldenberg H. Agni-Hyms—SBE, p. 61.
   4. Max Muller—Vedic Hymns—SBE.
   5. Geldner Karl F. Der Rig-veda, Vol. I, Hos 33, p. 88, ṛc 1.67.1.
   6. Skanda, Mudgala Com. VVRI, part I, p. 502.
   7. Veṅkaṭa—Ibid.
   8. Griffith, R., Hymns of the Rigveda Vol. I. p. 91.
15. —B 1. Sāy. comm. on 8.25.13—
अस्मदीयस्य धनस्य रक्षका भवन्ती इत्यर्थः।
   2. Griffith, R., Hymns of the Rigveda, Vol. II, p. 160.
   3. Geldner, K.F., Der, Rigveda, Vol. 34, p. 334.
   4. Skanda, Mudgala and Veṅkaṭa; Comm. in VVRI, part IV, p. 2683.
16. (i) 1. Sāy. comm. on 3.12.3—
इन्द्रमग्निं च युवां वृणे सोमपानार्थं इह कर्मकि आगच्छतं इति संभजे।

2. Oldenberg, H., "Agni-Hyms" SBE. No. XLVI, p. 263.
3. Geldner, K.F., Der Rigveda, Hos, Vol. 33, p. 349.
4. Skanda, Mudgala and Veṅkaṭa; Comm. in VVRI part III, p. 1323.

(ii) 1. Sāy. comm. on 3.12.5.—अहमपि इषः अन्नस्य त्वमार्थं इन्द्राग्नी युवां आ वृणे सर्वतः संभजे। पूणयामीत्यर्थः।
2. Oldenberg, H., The Agni Hyms, SBE. No. XLVI, p. 263.
3. Skanda, Mudgala and Veṅkaṭa; Comm. in VVRI, part III, p. 1323.
4. Geldner, K.F., Der Rigveda, Hos., Vol. 33, p. 349.

17. (i) 1. Sāy. Comm. on 5.50.1—तस्यानुग्रहात् सर्वे जनः धुम्नं धनं वृणति पुष्यसे पुष्ट्यै पर्याप्तं धनम्। (all the people get wealth on accounr of his favour.)
2. Geldner, K.F., Der Rigveda, Hos., Vol. 34, p. 55.
3. Skanda, Mudgala and Veṅkaṭa; Comm. in VVRI, Vol. IV, p. 1810.

(ii) 1. Sāy. Comm. 10.36-2-7.
2. Griffith—"We crave to day this gracious favour of the gods". Hymns to Rigveda, Vol. II, p. 433.
3. Geldner, K.F., Der Rigveda, Hos., Vol. 35, p. 187-188.
4. Skanda, Mudgala, Udgīta and Veṅkaṭa; Comm. in VVRI, Vol. IV, p. 1810.

18. (i) 1. Sāy. Comm. 10.91-8-9. हविषि समानमित् सहैव ऋत्विजः आ वृणते प्रार्थयन्ते।
2. Griffith, R., Hymns of the Rigveda, Vol. II, p. 521.

(ii) 1. Sāy. Comm. भद्रं वै शोभनमेव वरं वरणीयं दुःस्वप्न विनाशरूपं फलं वृणते सर्वे जनाः प्रार्थयन्ते।
2. Griffith, R., Hymns of the Rigveda, Vol. II, p. 598.
3. Veṅkata—
Skanda, Mudgala, Udgīta and Veṅkaṭa's comm. in VVRI, part VII, p. 3865.
4. Geldner, K.F., Der Rigveda, Vol. III, Hos. 35, p. 391.

(iii) 1. Sāy. किं चास्मिन् काले स्वपर्षासा स्वर्षातौसंग्रामे इन्द्रं वृणते संभजन्ते स्म।।
2. Griffith, R., Hymns of Rigveda, Vol. I, p. 575.
3. Geldner, K.F., Der Rigveda, Vol. II, Hos., Vol. 34, p. 114.

(iv) 1. Sāy. अवृणति प्रार्थयते प्रयुङ्क्ते।
2. Griffith, R., Hymns of Rigveda, Vol. II, p. 397.

3. Geldner, K.F., Vol. III, Hos. 35, p. 142.
4. Skanda, Mudgala, Udgītha and Veṅkaṭa's comm. in VVRI, part VI, p. 3252.
5. Velankar, H.D,. JUB, Sept. 1959, P. II, Hymns to Agni in Mandala X, p. 7.
6. Geldner, K.F., Der Rigveda, Vol. II, Hos. Vol. 35.

(v) 1. Sāy. comm. त्वां होतारं देवानामाह्वातारं वृणीमहे।
2. Griffith, R., Hymns of Rigveda, Vol. I, p. 483.
3. Geldner Karl, F., Der Rigveda, Vol. II, Hos. Vol. 34, p. 20.
4. Skanda, Mudgala, Udgītha and Veṅkaṭa's comm. in VVRI, part IV, p. 1697.

(vi) 1. Sāy. राजानं वाधताम् ऋत्विजामर्थाय अवृणि।
2. Griffith, R., Hymns of Rigveda, Vol. II, p. 182.
3. Geldner, K.F., Der Rigveda, Vol. III, Hos. Vol. 35.
4-5. Skanda, Mudgala, Udgītha and Veṅkaṭa's comm. in VVRI.

19. (i) 1. Sāy. यत् येन रथेन सूरिं स्तोतारं प्रति वरं श्रेष्ठं धनम् आ वहथः प्रापयर्थः।
2. Griffith, R., Hymns of Rigveda, Vol. I, p. 162.
3. Geldner, K.F., Der Rigveda, Vol. I, Hos. 33, p. 428.
4-5. Skanda, Mudgala, Veṅkaṭa comm. in VVRI, part II, p. 911.

(ii) 1. Sāy. इषं इष्यमाणमन्नरसादिकं वरं वरणीयं श्रेष्ठं अन्यदपि याग साधनं वरन्त प्रापयन्तु।
2. Griffith, R., Hymns of Rigveda, Vol. I, p. 195.
3. Geldner, K.F., Der Rigveda, Vol. I, Hos. Vol. 33, p. 197.
4. Velankar, H.D., JUB, Sept. 1963, P. II, Hymns to Agni in Maṇḍala I, p. 17.
5. Oldenberg.
6. Skanda, Mudgala, Veṅkaṭa comm. in VVRI, part II, p. 1000.

20. Burrow, T., The Sanskrit Language, Chap. IV, p. 124.
21. Modern Scholars like V.M. Apte also mentions two meanings of √vṛ—choose; protect or cover.
vide — JUB, Sept. 1950, Vol. XIX (new series), part 2, Apte V.M. p. 15.
22. 1. Sāy. comm. on the AV. 16.6.10.
2. Sātavalekar, D.V., on the Atharvaveda.
23. 1. Sāy. Comm. on 7.3.1.
2. Whitney keeps the form by question mark Whitney W.D. The Atharvaveda Saṁhitā, Hos. Vol. 7, p. 390, remarks in notes "This is a mechanical translation."

24. 1. Sāy. comm. 7.3.1.
    2. Sātavalekar, D.V. Atharvaveda Saṁhitā, part III, p. 24.
25. In Śukla YV. √vṛ also means to accept i.e. 1.13, 4.8; overcome—4.29; select. 27.3.
26. "Prāṇānām klṛptyai prāṇānām pratiprajñātyai— aṭhā etam varama-vṛṇīra." AB 1.2.1.
27. TS 6.1.5 mentions the same story parallel to AB 1.2.1, regarding Aditi's boon.
28. Payasyā—A mixture of boiled milk of a cow and little (a drop) curd.
29. KS 44.5
    Ātman is a chosen one. "by which he wins the Ātman."
30. Winternitz M.—HIL, Vol. I, p. 209.
31. Vide Winternitz M.—HIL, Vol. I, p. 197.
32. For the information about the boons and curses in the Rāmāyaṇa, vide—the article by Deshpande N.A.—Professor Birinchikumar Barua commemoration, Vol., p. 212.
33. MbH; Ādi parvan 1.16; quoted by Dange S.A. Legends in the Mahabharata, p. 1-2.
34. MbH. Vana Parvan. 3.131; 194 Anuśāsan Parvan—13.58.
35. Vide MbH. Vana Parvan 2903.
36. MbH. Vana Parvan, 38-40 (किरात पर्व)
37. Vide Kane, P.V., HDS, Vol. V, P. II, p. 909.
38. Vide Kane, P.V., HDS, Vol. V, P. II, p. 900.
39. Bhavabhūti also supports the thought in Malati-Madhava—
    सर्वेषां भगवतो भवितव्यतैव।
40. BHP. vide Kane, P.V.; HDS, Vol. V, P. II, p. 898.
41. BHP. 7.3.9 "कमण्डलु जलेनौक्षद् दिव्येनामोघराधसां"।
42. Vide Kane, P.V. HDS, Vol. V, P. II, p. 900.
43. Vide Kane, P.V. HDS, Vol. V, P. II, p. 896.
44. BRP, 1.11.2. चारिष्णुं धृतिमंतं च उभावंगिरसां वरौ"।
46. Compare to KATU.... नायं आत्मा प्रवचनेन लभ्यं......यमैवेष वृणुते तेनलभ्यः 1.2.23.

CHAPTER II

CONSPECTOUS AND BRIEF SUMMARY

SECTION I

It is well-known that Ups are the concluding portions of the Veda. They form a key-stone or the central arch of Indian philosophy and constitute one of the triple bases of Hindu Religion. Ups are called Vedanta because they form the crown of all knowledge.[1]

There are different Ups belonging to the each Veda and "there is a good deal of speculation concerning the number of Ups. Different estimates of their number have been given by the scholars : as they have been put by some scholars at as many 200. A popular edition usually contains 108 Ups.[2]

In some of the major, minor and later Ups there occur stories which have the theme of boons and they have generally the philosophical theme.

The following Ups deal with the topic under consideration :—

Major:—

1. CHU. 5.3.6 ; 2. BRU. 6.2.1-5;
3. BRU. 1.3.28; 4. BRU. 4.3.1.
5. KATU.

Minor :—

6. KAU. 1.1.; 7. KAU. 3.1;
8. MAU. 1.2.

Later Upaniṣads :—

9. Rāmottara-tāpinī 10. Gopālottaratāpinī (Vaiṣṇava)

11. Kaivalopaniṣad 12. Maitareya of SV.

13. Praṇava.

I. CHU. 5.3.6. introduces the famous dialogues of Pravāhaṇa Jaivali and Śvetaketu through which the knowledge about Pañcāgnividyā is expounded. It is clear that Upaniṣadic seers regard fire, air, water, as the source of elements. Here we meet with the doctrine of transmigration which is one of the basic concepts of Indian philosophy.

II. The BRU. 6.2.1-5. also deals with the Pañcāgni-vidyā. It is almost identical with the CHU. 5.3.6.

III. BRU. 1.3.28.

The portion under consideration deals with the Udgītha vidyā. In the purificatory hymns the Prastotṛ priest recites the chant; and while he recites it—the sacrificer recites the following three Yajus :—

"asato mā sad gamaya;
tamaso mājyotir gamaya,
mṛtyor māmṛtam gamaya."

When a sacrificer performs a Yajña he secures the fruit of it through the recitation of hymns of praise. It is stated in this context one should choose a boon. One should fulfil one's desires either for oneself or for the other.

IV. BRU. 4.3.1.

It deals with the teachings of Yājñavalkya. Here two prominent personalities viz. Janaka, a king—and

Yājñavalkya—a sage; stand out and with the help of rationational arguments the central idea of vedānta thought i.e. natute of Ātman is put forth. In it 'Ātman' appears as the ultimate source of all existence.

V. KATU.

The story of Naciketas expounds the nature of Ātman with illustrations etc. Naciketas goes to the Yama's abode because of his father's curse and obtains three boons from Yama. One of the important philosophical thought is nicely presented through the excellent and expert dialogue between Yama and Naciketas.

VI. KAU. 1.1.

The passage under consideration is a conversation between the king citra—the son of Gārgya and Śvetaketu with Āruṇi. It propounds what is called Paryaṅkavidyā. Citra expounds the philosophy :— "He (at the time of death) having reached the path of gods comes to the world of Fire (agniḥ) to the world of air (vāyuḥ), then to the world of water (Varuṇa) to the world of Indra, then to the world of 'Prajāpati', (Lord of universe), and at last to the world of Brahman.[4] Belvalkar S.K. classifies KAU in 4 units and comments : "The doctrine here taught is not new, sometimes it shows distinct echoes of texts like AA 2.1 of Bāṣkala—mantropaniṣad. But the manner of developing the idea is peculiar to it; and it reminds one of the closely reasoned argumentation of Yājñavalkya in BRU 4.3.5 though the conclusion here reached is on a somewhat lower philosophical plane, being psychological and epistemological rather than metaphysical.[5]

VII. KAU. 3.1.

This passage considers the doctrine of life-breath. The greatest gift that the knowledge of Indra being supreme Reality; is put forth through the dialogue of Pratardana and Indra. Pratardana, the son of Divodāsa went to the abode of Indra by means of battle and prowess.

VIII. MAU 1.2.

It deals with Brahmavidyā. It deals with the knowledge regarding the 'self' and the individual Soul; moreover the means of attaining unity with the Supreme Being, auesterity and meditation. It refers to the tri-murti concept—Brahmā, Viṣṇu and Śiva in 4.5.

Brahmā—Sūrya, Viṣṇu—Vidyut; Śiva—Agni. Some refers to the symbols of the trinity as time, water and fire. There are some scholars who think the trinity conception is as ancient as RV.[6]

IX. Rāmottaratāpinī 3.10-11. (RTU)

This Up forms the part of the AV and it is the second part of Rāmatāpinī Up. It mentions the unqualified Brahman. In this later Up, one comes across the ancient sages like Yājñavalkya, Bhāradvāja, Atri etc. The conversation of Yājñavalkya and Atri brings out that one acquires the liberation when a person realises that the Rāma is the supreme Being; He is the Paramātman. One attains this knowledge through the worship of Brahman—as Avimukta which is beween the two egestims, the taraka charater of the six-syllabled Rāma-mantra.

X. Gopālottara-Tāpinī (GU)

It belongs to the Av. The Gopālottara-tāpinī narrates the story of Kṛṣṇa and Durvāsas. The women of Vraja went to Kṛṣṇa and expressed their desire to go to Durvāsas who lived at the other bank of the Yamunā. The river gave way to the women of Vraja at the utterance of Kṛṣṇa's name. The name of Kṛṣṇa was considered to be a holy supreme one. The Up advices the recitation of Gopila's name to those, who are desirous of liberation.

XI. Kaivalopaniṣad—(KLU)

It is the concluding part of the Yv. The Up gives the meaning of the word 'Vara' as 'Variṣṭha'—that is the highest or 'Śreṣṭha'.

It is stated that Āsvalāyana approached Lord Brahmā and requested to fulfil his desire of geting the imparting of the Brahmavidyā to him. In this Up, it is clearly mentioned that the Brahmavidyā is the most excellent mystic. The knower of Brahman reaches Puruṣa when his sins are vanished. Brahmā shows the means i.e. śraddhā (faith), 'bhakti' (devotion) 'dhyāna' (meditation) and 'Yoga'; to get beattitude.

XII. Maitreya Upaniṣad of SV. 1.1. (MAIU).

It is divided unto three adhyāyas. It opens with a dialogue of the sage Śākāyanya and the king Bṛhadratha. The passage tells us about the seeker's inquisiton to have the knowledge of Ātman. The king performs a severe penance by fixing his eyes on the sun and keeping his arms uplifted. At the end of thousand days a muni called Śākāyanya is pleased with him and imparts him the knowledge about Ātman.

XIII. Praṇavopaniṣad—(PU)

It is published in the "unpublished upaniṣads". It deals with the Praṇava upāsanā.

"The authorship of the later Ups is attributed to some god or a sage. In case of seventy Ups the teacher is not mentioned but there is merely the mention that they belong to a particular Veda. A majority of these later Ups belong to the AV. This shows that Ātharvaveda sages play an important role in the teachings of the later Ups. The names of an ancient sages occur in the later Ups also as the authors of some of these works. This appears to be a purposeful attempt for obtaining authority for the new doctrines preached by the authors of later Ups.

Ātharvan-seers have followed the style of the ancient sages and at the same time advocated their new thoughts. A very vigourous activity in the field of construction and formation of the post vedic Purāṇic Hindu Religion seems to be carried on prominently under the influence of Atharvavedic teachers. By showing the great sages of the past also preached these new principles whether they may be about the devotation if the different gods or the Tāntric way of worship or the yoga; or Saṁnyāsa way of obtaining release from the worldly existence the later upaniṣadic writers have created a hollow of glory around these doctrines."[7]

"Jacob in his concordance of the upaniṣads" has used forty-five later upaniṣads. Sadhale Shastri has made use of two hundred and twenty three upaniṣads in his Upaniṣad-mahāvākya-Koṣa"[8] It is clear that the exact number of the later ups is not yet fixed.

Ups occupy a high spiritual esteem from the point of

view of thinkers of East and West. The study of ups shows that the Up touches every branch of knowledge.

They are not merely the works of the intellectual and logical arguments on the philosophy but they produce the knowledge of an ancient seer which he observes and realises; and he describes his realizaion in easiest words and in a simple manner, or in symbols or recommend bhakti of the deity concerned for the sake of all.

"It may be stated without any exaggeration that in the literature of the Ups Hindu philosophy, reaches the highest pinnacle of glory. It would also be no exaggeration to say that what Vyāsa said about MBH it is equally applicable to the Ups for whatever is contained in them is to be found in all the works of Hindu philosophy and whatever is not found in them is also not found in any part of Hindu philosophy.[9]

REFERENCES

1. Gurudas, "Glory of the Upaniṣads." Kalyana Kalpataru, Vol. 27, p. 27.
2. Gajendragadkar, P.B., "The Ten Classical Upaniṣads", Vol. I, Introduction, p. 52.
3. The following are the major or principal Upanishads :—Isa, Kena, Kaṭha, Praśna, Muṇḍaka, Māṇḍukya, Taitiriya, Aitareya, Chāndogya, Bṛhadāraṇyaka.
4. Radhakrishnan, S., 'The principle Upanishads, p. 156.
5. Belvalkar, S.K. and Ranade, R.D., Creative Period, p. 118.
6. Joshi, H.S., "Origin and Development of Dattātreya worship in India," Trinity ff, p. 15.
7. vide Desai, S.G., JUB, Sept. 1963, pp. 127-151.
8. vide Desai, S.G, "A later Up.—A Study", JUB, Sept. 1963, pp. 127-151.
9. Gajendragadkar, P.B., "The Ten Classical Upanishads", introducion p. 57.

SECTION II

I. CHU 5.3.6.

The story occurs as follows :—Once Śvetaketu—the son of Āruṇi went to the assembly of Pañcālās. He approached the king Pravāhaṇa Jaivali. At that time the king asked him five questions to taste his knowledge. The questions concerned about—(1) the place where men go from earth (2) their way of returning (3) from where the path is diverged (4) Why the 'water' is called 'man' in the 5th oblation.

Śvetaketu did not know the answers of all questions. Then the king said to him that how Śvetaketu replied that he was instructed by his father to the question of the king viz. 'Are you instructed?' The king offered him hospitality but Śvetaketu felt guilty and rushed to his father. It seems that it was a great insult to him in the presence of all the learned people. Śvetaketu angrily asked his father, "How did you tell me that you have been taught almost ; When I could not answer the questions of a king ?" It seems that Śvetaketu must be proud of his knowledge. Śvetaketu's father did not know them also. So Āruṇi went to the king as a pupil; though he was a Brahmin. Then the king explained the philosophical teachings what is called as "Pañcāgnividyā"—five fires viz. five fires are heaven, rain earth, man and woman. The five oblations are Śraddhā, Soma, rain, food and seed. Fire has five constituents—fuel, smoke, flame, live coals and spark.

The first question mentioned earlier is answered by mentioning the two paths. The second question is answered in CHU. 5.10.3-5. The two paths diverge (answer of a 3rd question) after reaching the moon.

The fourth question is answered in CHU. 5.10.8. The fifth question is answered by statement of Pañcāgnividyā.

II. BRU. 6.2.1-5.

This portion of Up. also deals with the discussion about five-fires. The fires are the same as mentioned in the CHU. 5.3.6 but the constituents of each of these fires differ slightly. The story deals with the conversation between Śvetaketu and the king-Pravāhaṇa Jaivali. In this passage it is stated that Śvetaketu, who being proud of his learning came to the assembly of Pancālās and saw there the king. Pravāhaṇa, being awaited upon by servants.The king asked him five questions but the questions are put in a slightly different form. The answers to these questions are identical to the answers in CHU 5.3.6; but there are some variations.

In this story the granter of a boon is a king viz. Pravāhaṇa Jaivali and the receiver of a boon is Āruṇi, Śvetaketu's father who mentioned as a wise and learned Brahmin.

III. BRU. I. 3.28.

The third Brāhmaṇa of the first Kāṇḍa introduces a beautiful parable which is connected with ritualism on the one hand and cosmology on the other hand.

At the beginning the story deals with the fight between gods and demons. Gods asked 'speech', 'eye', 'ear', 'mind' respectively to recite a Sāman for them. But all of them were unable to do so and gods were defeated by demons. At lasr it is the 'vital breath' which proved successful to conquerthe demons. This deity then purged the other deities of their evil and carried them beyond death. The vital Prāṇa is the essence of the limbs. He is spoken as Udgītha because he upholds the universe. Finally it is said that the sacrificial singer must recite the following lines when he begins to sing the Sāman:—

"Lead me from the unreal to the real;
Lead me from darkness to light;
Lead me from death to immortality".

If a person chants the prayer ih this strain, he is able to transcend the regions of illusions, darkness and death.

"The third part of the Ist Adhyāya takes us beyond Cosmology and drops us into ritualism once again."[1]

IV. BRU. 4.3.1.

The fourth Adhyāya which is known as Yājñavalkya Kāṇḍa describes the second dialogues between Yājñavalkya and the king Janaka.

It is told that Yājñavalkya came to Janaka thinking of himself not to speak with him. Though Yājñavalkya did not wish to say anything Janaka makes him to speak. Janaka asked him such a question which Yājñavalkya had permitted Janaka as a sort of boon when a discussion about Agnihotra took place formerly. This conversation of both these personalities points out an intellectual discussion about, what light a person have! Janaka puts a question "what serves as the light for man" ?, The querry of a king is satisfied by a answer in a simple manner. viz. "he has a light of the Sun". The whole Kāṇḍa deals with various arguments which concern about the Supreme light of man. While starting with the Sun, The Moon, Fire and Speech, Yājña-valkya ends his conversation by replying that the most Subtle entity is "Ātman". Sun, Moon, Fire etc, serve the function of light respectively.

This light is responsible for all the actions of a person. When Janaka goes on asking, "What is this Ātman?"; Yājñavalkya is forced to speak more and more till Janaka is satisfied with his logical and rational arguments.

S.K. Belvalkar remarks, "This queeey enables Yājñavalkya to weave together a number of philosophical luck-brations, which though seemingly sundered may yet be said to constitute a philosophical unity.[2]

The portion under consideration is one of the important and excellent passages in the Ups which inspire the different ācāryas to develop their philosophies. In this Kāṇḍa Yājñavalkya develops fully his own philosophy.

The last entity which functions as light for man viz. 'Ātman' is present in all the states : waking dream and sound sleep.Then follows the description of waking and the dream and sound sleep conditions. Yājñavalkya's views about the famous doctrine of Karma, viz. "what happens when a liberated soul passes away ?", are also expressed. In it the doctrine of Krma-mukti is rejected and sadyo-mukti is preferred.

V. KATU.

The KATU is one of the most widely read upaniṣ ads. It gives a vivid description of the nature of Brahman and the way to attain it. It begins with an ancient but an interesting story. A Brahman called Vājaśravas performed a sacrifice in which he gave away all his possessions. Amongst them there were few and feeble cows which were offered as a gift to priests. Vājaśravas' son—Naciketas was disturbed at the sight of such a gift which might lead to unthoughtful rewards that such a gift would be invalid. The giver of such unworthy gifts goes to the "Ananda-Loka"[3], and therefore having the knowledge of the Śastra's rule; Naciketas thought that it is a son's duty that he himself might be offered as a gift to the priest, and asked his father to whom he would be offered. When the Naciketas repeated the question his father became angry and exclaimed. "To death I give you".

The honest Naciketas took this as a command and gladly went to the abode of the Yama,—the god of death. But Yama was absent and so Naciketas had to wait at his door for three days before he came back. In order to pay off the compensation for the delay and discomfort; espeially to a Brahmin boy Yama promised him three boons.

As the first boon, Naciketas asked (1) "Let my father not felt angry or concerned at my absence". (2) His second wish "Tell me how my good works (iṣṭāpūrta) may not be exhausted" i.e. to know the nature of Fire-sacrifice, which would take him to the abode of the gods. Yama granted both the boons and he proved himself true to him. Moreover Yama instructed him regarding the method of sacrifice. "Now ask your final boon," said Yama. "When a man is dead," said Naciketas, "Some say he exists and others say that he doesn't; This I would like to know what is the truth about the Soul ?" Yama tried to divert his mind and tempted the boy from insisting on his last boon. He offered him all the pleasures in this world, and delights which are difficult to get on the earth e.g. gold, musical instruments elephants, cattle, horses, long span of life, beautiful damsels but all to him were of no purpose.

"I have seen the perishableness of these things, replied the Naciketas" and therefore he says "may those enjoyments remain with thee; keep them yourself. (KATU 9-1.20) "Tell what they ask for, concerning the next world, that only I wish to know and I will ask no other boon" (KATU 1.29) Thus Yama has no other choce and he proceeded to tell Naciketas the knowledge regarding the next world.

VI. KAU 1.1.

The passage under consideration is a conversation between the king Citra and the son of Gārgya and Śvetaketu—the son of Āruṇi. Once Citra desired to perform a sacrifice. At that time the king appointed Āruṇi as a priest but Āruṇi sent his son Śvetaketu (saying)—"Offer the sacrifice (KAU 1.1) so Śvetaketu went to the king. While seated on a seat the king asked him a question, viz. if there is any secret place where Śvetaketu would place him ! or if there is another world where he would tie down the king. Śvetaketu replied to the king. "I don't know ! let me ask the preceptor." After going to his father, Śvetaketu asked his father "What shall I reply him?" It seems that Āruṇi also did not know the reply. Āruṇi thought that the reply would be known in the assembly of the king. Āruṇi with his son approached the king taking samit in his hand. He utters the words "I am present". The king also showed respect to Āruṇi in the words : "O Gautam, you are honourable like a Brahmā !

since you have not shown pride. Come, I shall explain it to you." The king explained the philosophical teaching to him starting—"He (at the time of death) having reached the path of gods (devayāna) "Comes to the world of Fire (agni) to the world of Air, to the world of water, (Varuṇa) to the world of Indra, to the world of Prajāpati and (at last) to the world of Brahman." Further the portion under taken for study deals with the elaborate description of the world of Brahman which is called as "Paryaṅka". Citra's philosophical teachings are named as Paryaṅkavidyā.

VII.KAU 3.1.

The story tells that once Pratardana, the son of Divodāsa came to abode of Indra. Indra was pleased with his virtues like prowess and braveness and asked him to choose a boon. But the Pratardana refued to do so; and requested to Indra to choose it for him (i.e. Pratardana). Further it is also stated that Pratardana did not want to fulfil his own desire but prayed Indra to give such a knowledge which would do all good to humanity. There Indra disagreed with Pratardana by arguing that—a superior cannot choose for the Inferior. Then Pratardana also refused to have a boon. Thus Indra then after was compelled to impart the knowledge which would be useful for the whole mankind viz. know Him only because He is the truth and prāṇa; Prāṇa is prajñā i.e. Prajñātman etc.

VIII.MAU.

The Maitrayani Up introduces the story of the king

Bṛhadraṭha and the sage Śākāyana—who imparts the knowledge to the king, given by Maitri, and also to the Vālakhilyas by Prajāpati—Kratu.

The portion under consideration tells that the king Bṛhadraṭha performed severe penance in order to obtain Ātmajñāna. The king is shown as completely unattached towards worldly pleasures and had an earnest desire to know the Self. After some time the sage Śākāyanya happened to go to him and asked him to choose the desired object. At that time the king requested him to teach about the self since he was not an Ātmavit. The sage tried to withdraw him from asking such question. Here Śākāyanya advised the king to express any other desire. But the king prostrated himself at his feet and told him the transformable nature of the world, the uselessness of decaying body etc. At this moment the sage came to understand the indifference of the king towards this mortal world. Naturally the sage is pleased with him and said to the king that he was worthy of attaining his purpose and will and so explained him—"This indeed is thy self."[4]

The MAU also mentions threefold conception as Brahmā, Viṣṇu, and Śiva. Here the murti-traya is not to be considered as independent gods but they are the threefold manifestation of the one Supreme Being. By meditating on these forms one moves up higher and higher.

It also discusses 'Om'; three worlds worship of the Sun by means of Savitriprayer; eating of food as a sacrificial act; puruṣa and prakṛti; time and Yoga.

IX. RTU.

Rāmottara Tāpinī Up. has a dialogue of Yājñavalkya

and Atri about the well-known symbol "OM"— Afterwards the story is narrated : Once upon a time Rāma was pleased with the god Śiva and Rāma asked him to have a desired object and he also promised to fulfil it. In this Up. Rāma is considered to be the Supreme Being. He is to be worshipped while living in a 'Avimukta Kśetra'. In this Up. gods like the Śiva and the Rāma appear as the receiver and the granter of the boon. The humanic touch is given to them. The Śiva asked a boon : whosoever dies in Maṇikarṇikā in his temple or on the bank of the Ganges would have the liberation.

The Up. also discusses four morae of the sacred syllable OM as compared to Rāma, Lakṣmaṇa, Bharata, Śatrughna are considered to be three morae of OM and the half moroa is said to the Sītā.

X. GU.

Gopālottara-tāpinī Up. begins with the dialogue between the Durvāsas and Gāndharvi (Rādhā) in which Durvāsas answers the queries regarding the Kṛṣṇa. The Up. also gives full description of seven vanas and 12 forests in which the number of the gods reside.

Moreover it tells that Mathurā is the best sacred place, the favourite place of Kṛṣṇa. The Up. emphasises iconic worship and the Up. also points out that the iconic worship enables the man to be free from the death; to gain salvation. The Up. praises Lord Kṛṣṇa through out. This indicates the influence of the Kṛṣṇa-cult.

XI. KLU.

In the Kaivalya Up. through the speech of Aśvalāyana

and the Lord Brahmā, the principles of Vedānta philosophy are expounded. Lord Brahmā appears in an individual form and speaks about the Highest Self which is regarded as Śiva, Indra, Viṣṇu, Fire, Prāṇa. It is through the knowledge of Vedānta one knows him. People attain salvation not through Karma, Wealth, Progeny but through Sanyāsa alone. It is said that the recitation of the Up. is quite sufficient to get the reward viz. Kaivalya state.

XII. MAIU.[5]

This Up. deals with the dialogue between the king Bṛhadraṭha and the sage Śākāyanya, as is in the MAU. The king's complete indifference towards saṁsāra and his intence wish to know Brahman is expressed in the dialogue, wherein the king is addressed by Śākāyanya and the king requests him to enlighten him about Sattva (the state of sat or Brahman), the sage tries to divert his mind from that difficult question. But the king touches to the feet of Śākāyanya and expresses his sincere feelings that Śākāyanya is an expert in that particular field of knowledge to take him out of this mundane world. The king compares himself with a frog in a dry well as he remarks ; "I am drowned like a frog in a dry well, you are my refuge." (MAIU.).

XIII. PU.

Praṇavopaniṣad discusses the grammatical part of the "OM". 'OM' is considered as the most sacred syllable. Om-worship gives back the tejas.

REFERENCES

1. Belvalkar, S.K. and Ranade, R.D., Creative period, p. 183.

2. Belvalkar, S.K. and Ranade, R.D., Creative period, p. 205.
3. cf. Ś. Comm. on KATU. यास्ता एवं भूता गा ऋत्विग्भ्यो दक्षिणाबुद्धया ददत्प्रयच्छन्मन्दा अनानन्दा असुखानामेत्येतद्ये ते लोकास्तान्स यजमानो गच्छति।। vide Bhanu, C. G., Kaṭhopaniṣad, p. 285.
4. cf. "sarvam khalu idam Brahma."
5. Radhakrishnan takes Maitri or and Maitrayani Ups. belonging to one and the same branch of the black YV. He remarks "In some text it is assigned to the Sv. Op.cit. The Principal Upanishads, Radhakrishnan, p. 793 while Belvalkar takes Maitreya Up. of SV and Maitrayani of YV. as two distinct Ups. vide creative period, p. 123.

CHAPTER III

CHARACTERIZATION

In the Ups. under consideration, the upaniṣadic teachings centre around the nature of Ātman; the three states of the soul, the importance of Prāṇa etc. and all this is set forth by way of various conversations. At the Upaniṣadic time the method of imparting education was the Guru-Śiṣya-Saṁvāda. The disciple asks the questions and the guru answers his questions. Here a brilliant group of teachers and disciples is met with. These dialogues represent highly intellectual. Brahmins like Āruṇi Gautama, Yājñavalkya; and royal personages like Janaka, Pravāhaṇa Jaivali, Citragārgyāyaṇi, Bṛhadraṭha etc.

The Ups. present different characters as the seekers after the Highest Truth as a young pupil having just completed his pupilage like Śvetaketu; as a pedant ācārya like Āruṇi who was puzzled over a problem himself or sometimes he is a liberal and appreciative king like Janaka or a young boy, like Naciketas—full of enthusiasm for the metaphysical knowledge and who is proof against all kinds of tempations. Though yopung or old; rich or poor; the seeker is inquisitive about the Highest Truth.

On the other hand the Upaniṣadic teacher was such a worthy and respectful personality that everyone is tempted to bow down at his immense depth of knowledge; he was humble eager to teach; equally he was most patient and resourceful with his disciplines. Once the student successfully stood at their test, the response, the flow of knowledge that came from there was true and sincere of inward truth; it was the flow of real spiritual knowledge, The varied castes of personalities. Presented by these stories are true quite adequate to meet the demands of the creator's unique art.

In the Upaniṣadic times the Kṣatriyas took the leading part in the intellectual life. Kings were not only the patrons of learning but they knew some branches of knowledge which were unknown to Brahmins. This is illustrated by the following instances : 1. For the sake of knowledge the Brahmins never hesitated to bow down before a Kṣatriya. Āruṇi went to Pravāhaṇa—the king of Pañcāla with a view to learn Pañcāgni-vidyā.[1] There the king's remark "This vidyā did not rest with the brahmin family[2] is very suggestive. 2. In KAU[3] the citra-Gārgyāṇi's words. "You are worthy of Brahmin, O Gautama, Come here I shall make you know clearly" throws light on Āruṇi' praise-worthy character, a gallax personality; as well as the king Citra's hold over a particular vidyā that the person like Āruṇi approached him for instrucrion. It is evident from these facts that in the Upaniṣadic period the kings were not only learned scholars but also teachers. They were leaders in thought and culture. They also helped for the development of learning by holding conferences viz. a typical one is the videha philosophical conference held by the king Janaka. Thus the stories taken for study inform about the character's personality, nature, position in the society, depth of knowledge etc.

Uddālaka :

Uddālaka is one of the most prominent and important personalities in the Upaniṣadic literature.

He was a Kurupañcāla Brahmin and the son of Aruṇa; and the father of Śvetaketu. He belongs to Gautama family; in fact the whole family of Āruṇi was distinguished in history.

His family was most cultured and his literary fame extended over several generations.

He is mentioned as an authority on ritualistic problems and speculations.[4] The CHU. 5.3.6-10 refers from him as contemporary of Jaivali. He did not suffer from any complex, when he approached the king Jaivali. The KAU. describes him as a contemporary of king Citra-Gārgyāyṇi. Uddālaka was appointed as a chief priest in Citra's sacrifice but he deputed his worthy son—Śvetaketu to it. The BRU refers him as a contemporary of Yājñavalkya. It also appears that Yājñavalkya was one of his successors and also a disciple of Uddālaka. He was a teacher of his own son. Uddālaka was a life-long student who was old in years but everfresh and young to learn. This seems to be true when he becomes ready to go to Citra's assembly. When he found that the questions made by Citra to Śvetaketu are unknown to him also. Uddālaka is straightforward, he readily confesses his lack of knowledge to Śvetaketu.[5] ("I too did not know this, my son !"). He is openminded and modest. He goes to learn Vidyā to anybody; without feeling the superiority or inferiority for learning the knowledge. He was an earnest seeker of truth. Similarly he was an instense lover of Indian wisdom. He was very obedient, loyal student to carry out to the orders of his preceptor. He became ready to stay in Citra's house for a year, observing Brahmacarya, within a moment.[6] The charm of Uddālaka's personality remains in his simplicitude and in his quest of knowledge; so eager he was that Gārgyāyaṇi was surprised and he remarked : "You are worthy of Brahmin, the Divine knowledge, O Gautama."

His place in the history of Indian culture is thus indicated by Oldenberge : "When the time shall have come for the inquiries which will have to be made to create order out of the chaotic mass of names of teachers and other celebrities of the Brāhmaṇa period, it may turn out that the most important centre fot the formation and diffusion of the Brāhmṇa doctrine will have to be looked in Āruṇi and in the circles which surround him.[7]

MbH refers Uddālaka as a father of Śvetaketu and a disciple of Āyodhadhaumya; the story also mentions how Āruṇi got the name Uddālaka. Another story in MBH[8] is narrated in which Uddālaka is said to be father of Naciketas.

Śvetaketu Uddālaka Āruṇeya :

Śvetaketu was a grandson of Āruṇa and son of Uddālaka Āruṇi. He was initiated at the age of twelve and returned at the age of twenty-four having completed his education. He was very much proud of his learning but his father made him humble having shown him his lack of knowledge.

Yājñavalkya won him in the discussion on the occasion of sacrifice performed by Janaka[9]. Once he approached the king Pravāhaṇa but he was defeated there also.[10] He gained knowledge by opproaching the king Citra-Gārgyāyaṇi[11]. While commenting on the same passage (BRU 6.2.1.) Ś states, "the king had already heard of his pride for learning and wished to teach him a lesson."

The MbH[12] refers to Śvetaketu as a son of Uddālaka, born to his wife by one of his disciples. Śvetaketu was the first person who raised his voice against the evils of drinking and adultery by a Brahmin. There is a story in the MbH about the fact which prompted him to bring marriage system within a frame work of law.

The KAB describes Śvetaketu as an ācārya who made the rules of Yajña. He laid down definite rules and procedures for priests who would officiate in different capacities in Yajñas. He had suggested different customs and practices to be observedby brahmacārins and tāpasas.

MbH refers Śvetaketu and Naciketas as brothers.[13] Both

are from Gautama family. Son of Āruṇi[14] Āruṇeya is the family name of Āruṇi and Śvetaketu of Aupaveśi kula.[15] Prācin Caritrakośa mentions seven families those are called as Gautama viz. Aruṇa, āgniveśya, Uddālaka Āruṇi, Kuśri, Sāti and Hāridrumata.

Auddālaki is a name given to Śvetaketu and also to the Asurvinda[16] or Kusurubinda ācārya. Moreover in the Gautama family one person was known as Kuśri Vājaśravas[17] that is he may be the ancestor of Naciketas because Vājaśravas was Naciketas father's name. Hence Kuśri known as Vājaśravas—"who was famous for food" belongs to Gautama family because Hāridrumata, Uddālaka, Āgniveśya, Kuśri etc. are referred to be known as Gautama. Thus Śvetaketu belongs to Uddālaka family and Naciketas belongs to the Kuśri Vājaśravas family and therefore Śvetaketu and Naciketas can be called Auddālaki. The relationship between them can be drawn as follow according to the following "Pracin Carita Kośa."

Vājaśravasaḥ (also known as Uddālak)
|
Naciketas (Auddālaka)

Aruṇi (Uddālaka)
|
Āruṇi (Uddālaka)
|
Śvetaketu.

O
Vājaśravas — Aruṇi
Vājaśravas | Vājaśravasa (Kuśri) | Naciketas
Aruṇi | Āruṇi (Uddālaka) | Śvetaketu

So Uddālaka
Naciketas — Śvetaketu (MbH)

Therefore it can be concluded that Śvetaketu and Naciketas were related with each other but they were not closely related to each other. F.E. Pargiter mentions Uddālakas from two different Gotras i.e. one form Angirasa and the other form Ātreya.[18] Uddālaka or Uddālaki from Ātreya Gotra had a son called Naciketas, according to the view of Pargiter. Therefore Śvetaketu belonging to Aruṇa Aupaveśi family and Naciketas son of Uddālaka are not related to each other because the Gotras differ.

Pravāhaṇa Jaivali :

The name of the Pravāhaṇa Jaivali occurs in CHU 1.8.2, 5.3.1 and BRU 6.2.1. He was the son of Jivala and the king of Pañcāla.

In the JAUB he is mentioned as connected with some important rules and regulations that a priest should behave in a particular way.

He is associared with sāmans. He orders the priest to commence and halt the chanting of ṛcs. He also expresses his wish that they should sing sāmans with love and devotion.[19] He was one of the learned Kṣatriya kings who taught a Brahmin student. He had an assembly of learned scholars where Śvetaketu happened to go once, The king was a leading figure in the Pañcālas and famous for his special command over the Udgītha. He put several questions to Śvetaketu in the assembly and he failed to answer them. Hence Śvetaketu's father came to the court and submitted himself as a student.[20]

Ś states that the assembly of the Pañcālas was famous for learning. And the king was in possession of a particular branch of learning which was unknown to Brahmins. When the king started to explain to Āruṇi, the king expressed—"This Vidyā now will be known amongst Brahmins." This king was a specialist in subjects connected with mystery of life, death and immortality of the soul.

Janaka :

Janaka, the king of Videha is one of the most important personality in the ŚB, BRU; JaUBr. and KAU.[21]

Janaka is mentioned as the family-name of Videha or Nimi. It is the branch of a solar dynasty named from Nimi. The second man of the Videha is known as Mithi Janaka. He founded Mithilā-nagarī. All the persons from this dynasty are known as Janaka. They are mentioned in the Vedic and the Purāṇic literature. According to the TB he discussed philosophical themes with Yājñavalkya and Śvetaketu Āruṇeya. He is well known for his generosity and his keen interest in discussion about Brahman as the ultimate reality. The statemant of SB[22] shows that he reached the level of the Brahmin-philosophers in the attainment of knowledge.

He is known for his interest in philosophical problems. Once he taught Yājñavalkya in his earlier days.[23]

In the BRU. the name of the king Janaka occurs at various places.[24] He is associated with various philosophical conferences. A number of well-known philosophers and sages assembled at the court of Janaka and a debate was held on the interesting topics. Janaka's court was the centre of Vedic culture. He is always mentioned for giving the encouragement to the learned persons. He is always found in having the contact with the Brahmins of Kuru-Pañcālas like the sage Yājñavalkya, Śvetaketu etc. He is presented as a student of Yājñavalkya with a formal request.[25] He put some questions on the power of a boon granted by Yājñavalkya. In the conversation Janaka repeatedly requests him to instruct.

Though Janaka was a king he was unattached to worldly pleasures and possessions. He threw down the empire and himself at the feet of Yājñavalkya for the sake of Highest knowledge which destroys fear, pangs etc. completely.[26] To him philosophy was more important than sovereign powers.

In the Purāṇas Janaka is named as the king of Mithilā. He is regarded as one of the twelve sages who know the nature of dharma ordained by Hari. He is born from Nimi as per the Vedic reference but the Purāṇas make an innovation by observing that he was born by the churning of Nimi's body. The name of his son viz. Udāvasu is mentioned in it but the Purāṇas mentions his other relations as father of Sītā; father-in-law of Rāma etc. The Upaniṣadic reference viz. "Yājñavalkya won a prize for learning in Janaka's court" is elaborated in BRP. Once in the Aśvamedha sacrifice Janaka wanted to know the best amongst the scholars and declared a test prize of much gold, villages, servants and 11,000 cows.

Yājñavalkya :

He is a prominent authority on rituals in the SB and on philosophy in the BRU. In the SB he appears very frequently in the first five and the last four kāṇḍās as a noted teacher whose opinion is taken as authoritative.

Uddālaka was one of his teachers from whom he learnt Madhu-vidyā. Śvetaketu was one of his fellow-disciples. First Yājñavalkya was defeated by the king Janaka since he made Janaka to teach him ritualistic knowledge viz. Agnihotra. Afterwards Yājñavalkya grew up to be one of the most learned teachers of the time. He surpassed his own preceptor-Uddālaka in a disputation[27] in a vast assembly of scholars of the entire Kuru Pāñcāla country, held by king Janaka. In that conference he figured most eminent in philosophical problems. Ś comments on this portion and explains Gargi's speech; he says—"brahmodyam prati etattulyam na kaścit vidyate."[28] i.e. There is no equal to Yājñavalkya in describing brahman." He was a profound and unparalled scholar.

Once Janaka conducted a horse-sacrifice and he called an assembly to celebrate his sacrifice. In it he wished to find out the most superior one among the sages. The king declared a prize for a consumate scholar viz. one thousand cow to each pair of whose horns gold coins were fastened. Janaka announced that the one claimed to be eminent might come forward and take the cows with him. Here also Yājñavalkya proved his superiority over the the renowned scholars.

The BRU. 4.3.1 presents him as imparting the sacred knowledge of Brahman to the emperor Janaka. It is a discussion between them in the form of questions and answers viz. Janaka asked him "which is the light that guides us during the day time" the king's discussion goes on further. At this time the king was so much moved that he offered his entire-kingdom as a gift; with himself as an attendant.

Purāṇas mention that Yājñavalkya spent his major part of life at Janaka's court. He was also king Janaka's priest. The MbH[29] mentions him as a Brahmavādin and son of Viśvāmitra. The VAP[30] represents him as a son of Brahmavāh.

The BRP[31] describes the same episode and states that Yājñavalkya won the prize as renowned scholar in Janaka's assembly. He is associated with ritualistic philosophy. He is a philosopher. Upto the BRP he is prominent in the story. The story is not consistant fully but slightly differs viz. In BRP the number of cows increases upto 11000 than BRU.

Yama :

Yama is a god of death of Ṛgvedic antiquity. The RV[32] mentions Vivasvat and Sarayu as Yama's parents.

He appears as a teacher in KATU.[33] Naciketas being cursed by his father went to the residence of Yama and wished to know the highest truth. According to Naciketas Yama was the only person who knew about the Supreme Self and none other than him knew it fully well.[34] As a teacher he is reflected a strict person. At the beginning he examines the candidate well.

In Purāṇas Yama appears as a lord of Pitṛs. He punishes men after death according to their actions : sinful or sinless. He is a judge in the field of rewards. He rides on a buffalo. He is incharge of hells. Kāla and mṛtyu are his assistants. He was seen incarnate by Sāvitri, when he took away the life of her husband : Satyavat. Here he is kind enough to bless Sāvitri and returned the life of her husband. Generally he is figured as a terrific person and a ruler of the Yamaloka. When the life-span of a being is over, Yama sends agents who take the soul to Yamapuri. From there the holy souls are sent to Vaikuṇṭha and the sinful one to different hell.

Maitri :

Maitri was a famous teacher. He was a great Ātmavit who imparted instructions to his disciple Śākāyanya. He was a well-known exponent of the highest secret of the Ups.[35]

Naciketas :

Naciketas was a well-known son of a ṛṣi. He is also called Gautama[36] and is a son of Vājaśravas; Vājaśrava is a family name of Kuśtī and Naciketas. In KATU[37] he is called Auddālaka, i.e. to say a son of Uddālaka Gautama.

The earliest reference of Naciketas is found in the Rv. Yama-sukta.[38] According to Sāyaṇa the Yama-sukta denotes Naciketas by the vocable "Kumāra" further this sukta tells that the son (Kumāra) of Vājaśravas went to Yama's abode to carry out the command of his father and he made Yama pleased with him and then Naciketas returned.

The TB elaborates the story of Naciketas in which Naciketas's father is said to have performed Viśvajit sacrifice. The sacrifice needs all the possessions to be offered to the priests. In this account Naciketas, though a young boy, is depicted as thoughtful Kumāra.

Naciketas also tried to prevent his father from offering feeble and old cows as gifts. Again and again the boy is seen to be asking only one question (i.e. Kasmai mām dāsyāmi ?) even though his father neglected his question at first. Naciketas is depicted as young but matured well versed, sincere and devoted kumāra. He is not afraid of death, when he carried out his father's command.

In KATU the same story is presented in detailed with a philosophical background. Herein the young chap is represented as thinking of his father's anger all the while, when he asked for his first boon. Similarly he remained steady and unmoved when Yama offered him the delights and enjoyments like gold, cattles, sovereignity over the earth; musics etc. His nature is stead-fast, firm and the charming attractions had no effects on him. He did not hanker after praise. All the time he insists on Yama to impart to him the knowledge about 'Self'. He is interested in knowing the highest principle and nothing else.

Naciketas is mentioned in MbH—Anu parvan Chap. 71 in a different context. The story is related to him from TB and KATU.[39] In MbH. he is presented as a sage of olden days and son of Uddālaka. He had the life of a hermit for a long time serving upon his father. Once his father cursed him, when he did not bring flowers, samits etc. from the forest and was taken to Yamaloka. Here the purpose of going to Yamaloka and the reason of his father's anger differ from those in the TB and KATU. Yama advised him when he came back. Naciketas became a great scholar.

Citra-Gārgyāyaṇi :

The character of the king Citra-Gārgyāyaṇi occurs in the KAU 1.1. He was one of the most learned Kṣatriya kings.

Citra is the name of several persons. The Rv[40] contains a Dānastuti of a prince named Citra. The legend attributes this to Sobhari and describes Citra as a king of rats.

In the KAU Citra figures as a teacher of Uddālaka Āruṇi. He is the knower of some secret vidyā. He is a contemporary of Śvetaketu and Āruṇi.

Bṛhadraṭha :

King Bṛhadraṭha belonged to the family of Ikṣvāku. Pondering over the transient nature of the world he relinguished his throne and he went to the forest to perform severe penance[41]. One day a sage called Śākāyanya appeared before him and instructed him about the Highest Self.

The Purāṇas mention a number of kings named Bṛhadraṭha. One of them belonged to the Maurya family as (1) a son of Śatadhanvan; (2) a son of a Devavrata of Sahadeva family; (3) as a father of Kuśāgra etc. The king Bṛhadraṭha mentioned in MAUP may be related to one mentioned in the VAP,[42] in the VP Bṛhadraṭha was the son of Bṛhadraṭha and the father of Bṛhadkarma. The Ikṣvāku line kings originated from him. Bṛhadraṭha, the son of Śatadhanvana went to the forest and became an ascetic. He practised penance to attain heaven. He wished to know the secret of Eternal truth from Śākāyanya.

Śākāyanya :

He is mentioned as a having lusture like a burning fire in MAU. He went to the king Bṛhadratha when the latter performed severe austercity. The sage taught him the Brahmavidyā.

Indra :

Indra is favourite god of Vedic Pantheon. He is invoked with highest attributes throughout the Rv. Nearly one fourth of the Ṛgvedic hymns celebrate the glorification of this god.

He is praised separately as well as praised with other gods. Indra is not a natural phenomena as Agni, Surya, Maruts, Varuṇa. On the contrary it presents cosmic power. He is surrounded by the myths than any other god of the Rv. Indra is a leader of Vedic Aryans and a dragon killer, According to one view the figure Indra indicates the personification of thunderstorm; the conquest with demons of drought and the release of waters or the winning of light is frequently described. Most of the descriptions of Indra are woven round Indra-Vṛtra combat and the victory of Indra over Vṛtra. It is said that heaven and earth trembled with fear when he smote Vṛtra with his thunder-bolt. A Vedic seer proclaims the heroic deeds of Indra thus : He is said to have torn as under the mountains and released the waters or cows imprisoned in the caves."

He stands in the middle region. Indra's personality grew among Vedic people. It reflects the Vedic religion. It indicates the personification of human and super-human element. It presents the most lively and attractive picture. Indra's physical features like head, arms, hands, belly, lips moustache etc. are described in the connection with his powers of drinking soma. The epithets like "Maghavan", "Vasupati" suggest Indra's generosity bountifulness. The attributes of Indra are of physical type but he is a dreadful, invincible person; an irresistible warrior whose mighty powers win victory always.

In the Brahmaṇa period Viṣṇu gains ascendency. In the purāṇic period Indra's position declines. He became subordinate to Brahmā, Viṣṇu, Maheśa. The Viṣṇu—worship gradually increased in the Purāṇic period.

In KAU 3.1 Indra is presented as instructing the supreme knowledge to the king Pratardana. He bestows such knowledge which would be beneficial to the whole mankind.

Indra appears as demon in the Iranian Culture[43].

Pratardana :

The king Pratardana is mentioned in KAU 3.1. In the RV he is said to be a Kāśirāj Daivodāsi. He is a seer also[44]. His son is Bhāradvāja. In the SB[45] he is referred to as having discussed the faults in the sacrifice in the Naimiṣāraṇya. He attained the Indraloka after his death.

In the KAU 3.1 he is mentioned as the son of Divodāsa, the king of Kāśī. He went to the abode of Indra by means of prowess and battle. Indra was pleased with his bravery and promised to bestow on Him a boon. Pratardana was wise enough to secure the best knowledge from Indra having said that Indra should stick to his words and bring harmony in words and actions.

In Purāṇas[46] Pratardana is also mentioned as a king but the information regarding his parentage follows there in more details than the RV and the Ups. He is a king of the Puru dynasty. He was the son of the daughter of the king Yayāti. He ruled the country after making Kāśī as his Capital. Pratardana's mother's name was Mādhavī, Yayāti's daughter and his father was Divodāsa. Once Pratardana happened to come across on his way his grand father viz. Yayāti, who had fallen from Svarga.

Rāma :

Rāma is a name of king in the Rv[47].

In the Epics and Purāṇas he is glorified with vivid pictures of his heroism. In the later Ups like Rāmarahasya and Rāmottaratāpini Rāma is developed as a god. He is regarded as and incarnation of Viṣṇu. All the epithets of Viṣṇu are applied to Him; and he is worshipped as a deity by number of people even in the twentieth century. In Rv. it is told that Rāma is Brāhman. Rāma is mentioned as a Vāsudeva in the vyuha. Similarly Rāma is described as 'Turya' among four states in the line of Vedānta. That means Rāma is described and praised in both ways (1) in the Vedānta philosophy (2) in the traditional cult of Bhakti that is by the Rāmānuja point of view. Lakṣmaṇa; Bharata; Śatrughana and Sītā are mentioned to be the parts of Rāma. Sītā, the consort of Rāma is the Pṛakṛti. Rv describes that Sītā, the delightful one is the source of things in the world. Lakṣmaṇa, Bharata and Śatrughna also constitute their roles and Viśva, taijasa and Prājña conditions when Rāma described as the most important state viz. Turya, in the line of Gaudapāda. They equally share different parts along with Rāma when Rāma is mentioned as "OM". Rāma is considered as ardhamātrā of "OM", without which the worship of "OM" could not be completed. Rāma is worshipped with the help of mantra.

Rāma worship was raised to the highest rank to the such an extent that RU[48] mentions all other cults i.e. those of Gāṇapatyas, Sāktas, Vaiṣṇavas are not meritorious as compared to Rāma worship.

In Purāṇas Rāma is known as a son of king Daśaratha. He is known for his rightousness and truth. He was born in the Ikṣvāku race and was a brother of Lakṣmaṇa, Bharata and Śatrughana[49].

He killed many demons like Mārica, Rāvaṇa, Khara and Kumbhakarṇa. Along with his wife viz. Sītā, Rāma spent a forest life in obedience to his father's command. He is presented as a vigourous king; led a life as a celibate; give joy and happiness to the subject. He also performed sacrifices by giving all his kingdom as gift.

Kṛṣṇa :

Kṛṣṇa occupies prominent place in epics and Purāṇas to a great extent. Kṛṣṇa is a hero in Bhāgavata Purāṇa. He is considered to be an incarnation of the supreme god Viṣṇu.

Although Rv[50] represents Kṛṣṇa as the name of a sear, there are few references of Kṛṣṇa or Kṛṣṇas in Rv compared to Purāṇas. The authorship of Rv[51] which regards Kṛṣṇiya as a Patronymic form appears to be derived from the Kṛṣṇa. The Lord Kṛṣṇa has a very close relation with the Vedic figure viz. Indra[52]. Indra, almost serves as a model on which some of the later Kṛṣṇa stories were developed. Kṛṣṇa is identified with Indra the most prominent and popular god of the Indo-Aryans. Although the figure Kṛṣṇa does not appear in the hymns of the Veda, some of the importants traits, associated with him are conspicuously present there marks. In the Vedic times Varuṇa was worshipped mostly, then Indra surpasses the god Varuṇa; then after the Indra worship is turned into the Viṣṇu's glorification. The Viṣṇu is regarded as the most supreme god afterwards. He surpasses all the other gods of the Veda. And the Kṛṣṇa is regarded as the incarnation of the Viṣṇu. Thus the Lord Kṛṣṇa may be identified with the Indra of the Rv. The form Kṛṣṇa compounded with Aṅgirasa is mentioned in KAB.

The CHU[53] speaks Kṛṣṇa as a son of Devaki; as well as a student of Ghora-Aṅgirasa. Several modern scholars like Grierson-Garbe and Von Schroeder indentify this Kṛṣṇa with later Kṛṣṇa of Purāṇic times. There are much contradictory views regarding the identification of Kṛṣṇa of CHU and Kṛṣṇa of Purāṇic tradition[54]. Scholars like R.G. Bhandarkar, A.D. Pusalkar and Benjamin[55] deal and discuss the Kṛṣṇa problem.

The Purāṇas represent Kṛṣṇa as a descendent of Yadava family, who spent his childhood in Gokula and then spent his life in Dvārkā. MbH and Purāṇas call him Vāsudeva. He was a reality to the ordinary minds of the people. The stories about Kṛṣṇa as a killer of Kaṁsa. Jarāsandha; Slayer of a dragon are sung beautifully in Purāṇas. Then Kṛṣṇa is raised to the rank of supreme divinity. Kṛṣṇa an incarnation of Nārāyaṇa reaches the highest position within the Vaiṣṇavas as in BHP.

At the later Upaniṣadic period a separate cult of Kṛṣṇa as a supreme deity might have developed. He is regarded as a Pūrṇāvatāra of Viṣṇu in mortal form. Kṛṣṇa's character is reflected as a human hero rather than his divine form. He acts according to the human motives. In the GU Kṛṣṇa is identified with the Brahman. He is described as unqualified i.e. he is not a enjoyer of the fruits. He is the witness of all the acts. Similarly the bodily description of Kṛṣṇa follows in GU[56]. It is said : Those who worship Kṛṣṇa having fourhands with the Conch, Shell, bow, and lotus in Mathurā get emancipation. Similarly GU describes the brightness of Kṛṣṇa's garments, garland of Kaustubha jems, earings etc. Mere utterence of Kṛṣṇa is the Saviour of distressed souls.

Śiva :

The worship of Śiva goes back to very early times. It was current under Rudra's name among the Vedic people. Formarly Rudra was prayed in various hymn[57] and in some of the hymns he was asked to protect the children from the effect of diseases. He is often spoked as the best physician, similarly he possesses the power of healing remedies. Rudra is aweful and terrible god in the Ṛgvedic times. He is represented as having brilliant shafts which spread over heaven and earth.[58] Rudra is always associated with Maruts. Rudra's phenomenon is indicative of destructive energy.

"In the YV and AV Rudra had attained the nature of a benignant God the whole majesty of the god-head[59] Rudra's glory appears in its peak at the time of Brāhmaṇas. In the later time that is in the period of Epics and Purāṇas he becomes prominent and widespread. Rudra's dreadful and destructive character is appeased. He appears as beneficient saṁkara auspicious (Śiva).[60]

N.J. Shende opines that the cult of Śiva is earlier than Kṛṣṇa cult. The germs of Śiva cult exists even before the Vāsudeva Kṛṣṇa cult was more popular; and the Śaiva Ups pour its loving adoration on Rudra-Śiva. Similarly when Vāsudeva Kṛṣṇa came into field, the germs of Bhakti speedily developed towards Kṛṣṇa.[61]

The Kaivalya Up glorified Śiva as the supreme lord of the universe. The Up advises that the Saṁnyāsin should devote himself to the meditation of Śiva for getting emancipation. Śiva is described as eternal principle; he pervades all living and non-living beings. He is creator, protector and destroyer of the world. Usually in the Ups. the supreme entity is "Brahman" when is described as Nirguṇa-nirākāra but it is shown as Saguṇa having forms viz. three eyes and dark blue throat[62] in latter times. Śiva is said to have thousand names. He is considered as a master of gaṇas and bhūtas. He is well-known for his liberality in granting boons. He is a great Yogin and the residential place of Him is Kailāsa.

Gautama :

Gautama is a common patronym as well as it is applied to a descendent of Gotama to Aruṇa, Uddālaka, Aruṇi, Kuśri, Sāti, Haridrumata etc.

Gotama Rahugana is mentioned in the RV.[63] He figures as purohita or a family priest of king Mathava Videgha in SB. Gautama / Gotama is a famous seer among Rāhugaṇa. Small Gaṇas were grown up at the time of Bhāradvāja. 20 Sūktas are alloted to Gautama in his name. Gotama obtained wealth having pleased Aśvins.

JAUB, TAB also mentions the names as Gotama and Gautama.[64,65]

REFERENCES

1. CHU 5.8, BRU 6.2.7.
2. BRU 6.2.8.
3. KAU. 1.1.

4. SB. 1.1.2.11; 2.2.1.34; 3.3.4.19; BRU 3.5.1; CHU 3.24; 5.3.6-10.
5. His speech. CHU 5.3.6ff.
6. KAU 1.1.2.
7. Oldenberg's remark quoted in "The History of Buddhistic philosophy.", p. 396 (n).
8. MbH. Anu Parvan. Chap. 71.
9. SB. 11.6.2.1.
10. BRU. 6.2.5. ff.
11. KAU. 1.1.
12. MbH. Śanti Parvan. 35.22.
13. vide, Siddhesvarashastri Citrāvas, "The Prāchin Caritrakoṣa".
14. Naciketas is called Gautama & Auddālaki in KATU. KATU. 1.1.10-11.
15. SB. 10.3.4.1.
16. JB. 1.75.
17. SBr. 1.16, PB. 22.15.10.
18. Op. cit. Pargiter, F.E., Ancient Indian Historical Tradition, p. 327.
19. Ortel H. JAUB. 1.38.4
20. CHU 5.3.6 and BRU. 6.2.4.
21. SB 11.3.12; 4.3.20; BRU 3.1.1; 4.1.4; 2.1; 4.3.1 Jai. Br. 1.19, KAU. 4.1; TB. 3.10.9.9.
22. SB. 6.2.10.
23. SB. XI 6.2.
24. BRU. 2.1.1; 3.1.1; 4.3.1; 4.3.38 etc.
25. BRU. 4.3.1.
26. BRU. 4.3.24
27. BRU. 3.7.1.
28. ŚBH on BRU. 3.8.12.
29. MbH. Anu. Parvan. 4.5.51.
30. VAP. 60.4.1.
31. BRP. 1.2.30.36 ff.
32. RV. 10.14.5.
33. KATU 1.1.20.
34. KATU 1.1.22.
35. MAU 2.1.3.
36. SB. 10.5.5.1; TB. 3.11.8.1, 1.30.103.
37. KATU 1.1.11.
38. Rv. X. 35.
39. The story of Naciketas is discussed in "Some Remarks on the 'Naciketas legend". Vide Dr. S.G. Kantawala, Ludwick's felicitation Vol., p. 293.

40. Rv. 8.21.18.
41. MAU 1.1.
42. VAP 99.281; VP 4.18.22.
43. vide : Burrow, T., "Journal of the Royal Asiatic society", 1973 (London) : "The Proto-Indo-Aryans", p. 123-140.
44. Rv. 9.96; 10.179.2.
45. SB. 2.6.5.
46. VAP 99.281.
    VP 4.18.82.
47. Rv. 10.193.14,15.
48. RU. 6.4.
49. BHP 1.12; 2.7.23-25; and MP 12; 50-51.
50. Rv. 8.25.34.
51. Rv. 8.86; 1.116, 1.117.
52. vide Benjamin Solis, "The Kṛṣṇa cycles in the Purāṇas", p. 17.
53. CHU 3.17.6.
54. vide, Pusalkar, A.D., Studies in Epics and Purāṇas Historicity of Kṛṣṇa ff., p. 49.
55. op. cit. Benjamin Solics, "Kṛṣṇa cycles in the Purāṇas.
56. GU 61-63.
    "श्री वत्सलाञ्छनं हृत्स्थं कौस्तुभं प्रमया युतम्।
    चतुर्भुजं शश्वचक्रशार्ङ्गपद्मगदान्वितम्..........।।"
57. Rv. 7.46.2, 7.46.3, 1.43.4 etc.
58. Rv. 7.46.3.
59. vide Shende, N.J., "The Religion and Philosophy of the Atharva-veda", p. 243.
60. For an account of the origin and growth of Saivism, vide e.g. Bhandarkar, R.G., op.cit., pp. 102ff.
61. vide Shende, N.J., "The Religion and Philosophy of the Atharva-veda", p. 242.
62. KLU 1.7.
63. RV. 1.78.5.
64. JAUB—
    (i) 1.14 गोतमस्य मनर्यि मनोऽपक्रान्तः कुर्वीत।
    (ii) 3.44 अथ गौतमम्। गोतमो वै राहूगणोऽकामयत.........उभय उपासते।।
65. (iii) 2.218.

CHAPTER IV

PHILOSOPHICAL DOCTRINES

The stories under study deal with various views about the transcendental world. The main theme of Ups. is the omnipresent, omniscient, omnipotent Brahman. They stress that Brahman or Ātman is all-powerful and it is the underlying principle of the universe. It is its power that keeps natural objects viz. Sun, moon, stars, earth etc. in their proper order. all beings dwell in it and it is present in all beings. The Ātman is the support of everything. The same thought is stated in BG[1] and Iśa. Up.[2] i.e. Ātman is inside as well as outside of the beings. It is subtle.

Because Ātman is subtle, He is inside as well as outside of all the things. The Ātman is formless, spotless and sinless. He is pure, inscrutable and immutable. The knowledge of the Ātman leads to fearless state of mind. The person enjoys bliss. As a means to realisation the Ups. Lay stress on desireless action, control of mind and performance of tapas. Ups speak the works done devoted to the God again and again. It is a duty of person to act for the society. Iśa. Up.[3] Suggests also the desireless action. 'anāsakta karman' i.e. when a desire for reward is given up and the action is devoted to him, such desireless actions do not bind a person, do not cling to a man.

If the activities of life carried on with the remembrance that all works belong to Almighty; a person is freed from the bondage of karman.

CHU. 5.3.6.

I. The CHU speaks about the jaivali's speculation through the interesting dialogue between Jaivali and Uddālaka Āruṇi. At the beginning the dialogue points out Śvetaketu's iinability to reply king Pravāhaṇa Jaivali, when Śvetaketu, Āruṇi' s son approached to the king.

It should be noted that Śvetaketu was not told to go to the king by anybody as in the case of Naciketas. The CHU 5.3.6 does not mention the reason why Śvetaketu approached the king compared to KATU[4] viz. Naciketas went to the abode of Yama because his father offered Naciketas to Yama. It was obligatory to Naciketas while in the case of Śvetaketu, no one forces him to go to the assembly of the king Pravāhaṇa Jaivali; however Śvetaketu went to the king's assembly but he was unable to answer the questions of Jaivali; so he returned and related the incident to his father. Āruṇi and he did not know the answers to the questions. Āruṇi then approached to the king as a pupil, though he was a Brahmin. The king jaivali offered him hospitality and asked him to have a boon regarding the mānuṣavitta (material prosperity). But Āruṇi did not accept the king's offer and Āruṇi wished to know the answers of the questions which were put to his son. Āruṇi desired to seek the philosophical knowledge; he had all the material prosperity. At this time Pravāhaṇa hesitated to answer him for the time being because the king knew this vidyā which Kṣatriyas only had. While knowing the modest and simple attitude of such a learned Brahmin, the king asked him to live as a Brahmacārin for a whole year. After the period was over the king explained the philosophical teachings.

This story suggests that for the realisation of a boon Brahmacarya is required. The granter of a boon is Pravāhaṇa, a king; and a receiver of the boon viz.

Śvetaketu's father Āruṇi is Brahmin by caste. The receiver here is on a higher social level. Though Pravāhaṇa was a Kṣ atriya king, he possessed a secret knowledge. Usually a kṣ atriya was meant for ruling the society. The king's duty was to protect the people. But here in the story taken for study reflects that kṣatriyas were repositary of knowledge. It means teaching and learning was not the monopoly of Brahmins only. Here jaivali, though a king is seen oblizing Āruṇi by giving this vidyā. The king says:" I am telling this vidyā now and it is only among kṣatriyas and from you it will spread among Brahmins.[5] The remark of jaivali also points out that the caste system was followed by people at the Upaniṣadic time.

The CHU states that if a man meditates of five elements viz. (1) Heaven (dyuloka) (2) rain (parjanya) (3) Earth (pṛthivi) (4) Man (puruṣa) (5) Woman (Yoṣā); he will go along the northrn path. These elements are to be considered as fires. In these five fires the following five oblations are offered viz.—śradhā, soma, varṣā, annam and retas respectively. These five offerings produce five kinds of results i.e. Soma, varṣā, annam retas and garbha respectively. The description of the fires is as follows :

(1) Dyuloka : The heavenly region is fire. The sun itself is fuel, the rays are smoke; the flames are the days and the sparks are the stars. In this first fire the gods offer faith as the oblation from which soma arises.

(2) Parjanya : The rain is the fire and the air (Vāyu) is the fuel; the cloud is the smoke; the lightening is the flame; the thunder bolt is the coal; and the rumblings of clouds is the sparks. In it the Soma is offered as the oblation. The result of the offering rises shower.

(3) Pṛthivi : The earth is the fire, herein the year is the fuel; the space is the smoke; the night is flame; the quarters the sparks.

(4) Puruṣa : The man is the fire and the speech is the fuel; the breath is the smoke, the tongue is the flame; the eyes are the coals and the ears constitute the sparks. Foods is offered here as the oblation in it results into the seed.

(5) Yoṣā : The woman herself is the fire; in this context the sexual organ is the fuel, the vulva is the flame; the art done within is the coals, whereas the pleasures are the sparks. In this context the seed is offered as the oblation which gives rise to foetus. Thus in the fifth oblation a man arises out of water.

According to the jaivali's eschatalogical view when a man dies, the dead body is carried to the funeral fire; it takes a subtle form when it is burnt. Now if the man has practised tapas with sincere devotion, or if he is from the category of gods, his soul passes from light to light till it reaches Brahman. The souls journey may be shown as follows :

light
↓
day
↓
bright half of the moon
↓
six months when the sun goes to the north
↓
year
↓
sun
↓
moon
↓
lightening
↓
amanava-puruṣa

This is the gods' path that leads to the Brahman. This process of ascent of the soul carries the soul to immortality as distinguished from the process of rebirth.

If a man performs sacrifices and works of public utility, his way of journey is different. He goes to:

smoke
↓
night
↓
dark half of the moon
↓
six months when the sun goes to the south
↓
world of fathers
↓
ethereal region
↓
moon

This path is named as Pitṛyāna. The soul stays at moon till his reward of works is exhausted; then his back journey starts and the downward.

Smoke→mist→cloud→rain→rice→corn→herbs and trees→food→seed→man. If the man's conduct is good he gets the birth of a Brahmin, Kṣatriya, Vaiśya, otherwise he is born as a dog, cat or a cāṇḍāla. This path brings the soul back to the cycle of rebirth.

Thirdly if the man is a thief, steals gold, drinks or kills brahmin, his soul is thrown into the hell.

Jaivali's philosophic consumption of rebirth is propounded for the first time. The lower creatures live and die continuously.

Jaivali insists on that the inner vision or the knowledge

is not sufficient but the man's spiritual progress should remain consistent throughout his/her life.

The BRU 6.2.5ff propounds the same doctrine. the teaching of the CHU and BRU seems to be similar on pañcāg-nividyā but there are some minute significant variations and they are as follows :

1. The questions which were put by the king jaivali, are slightly different but they convey one and the same idea.

2. The five fires are same but the constituents of each of these fire differ. There are differences in the text of the CHU 5.3.6 ff. and the BRU 6.2.5 ff.[6]

The CHU explains five fires, while as BRU as one more fire to it i.e. It deals with six fires. It is told that when a man is cremated, the lusturous soul is produced from the cremation fire and this fire serves as the altar. This goes to the world of the gods or to the world of the fathers according to his deeds. The fruit of pañcāgnividyā is also given after the description of it. The CHU says that the person, sho knows five fires, is not affected by any kind of sin eventhough he is associated with it. He is pure and clean and obtains the world of the blessed[7].(CHU.5.10.10.). The aspirant becomes holy by realising the significance of the pañcāgnividyā.

The BRU throws more light on the results pertaining to five-fires. Those who know this pañcāgnividyā and those who meditate with faith upon the Brahman in the forest,

reach the deity identified with the flame from him the deity of the day, then to fortnight, in which moon waxes, then deities of six months-northern-sun-being-created from the mind (of hiraṇyagarbha) comes and conducts then to the world of hiraṇyagarbha. They attain perfection, eternal life and live there.

Both the Ups. Reveal the doctrine of five fires. If the

teachings of the both Ups are put together,The full eschatological teaching of Pravāhaṇa can be formed. Pravāhaṇa stresses the main idea namely that there are two paths for men who have passed their life either for public utility or performed auesterity in the forest; and those who led a good and spiritual life. One is devayāna or what the BG calls as arcirmārga and the other is the pitṛyāṇa i.e. dhūma-mārga.

CHU and BRU—pañcāgni-vidyā

The grandson of Aruṇa viz Śvetaketu came once to the assembly of the Pañcālas to display his learning (CHU).

The Pañcālas were famous for learning, The Śvetaketu approached the king with a proud idea of defeating his assembly and thereby conquering the royal court. (BRU).

In the BRU the king offers him a gift [8] "The king addresses him that he will offer a boon (present) to revered Gautama. The BRU 6.2 does not mention what sort of present jaivali was going to offer to Āruṇi while the CHU 5.3.6 mentions it clearly. The king in the BRU never mentions so, perhaps the king might have wished to say that as a general practice when a Brahmin happened to see a king. The king gave some gifts to the guest in any form, e.g. wealth, cows, horses, servants, land etc. and thereby used to make him happy. Since long the practice is running and by offering a gift to a Brahmin the donor gains the merit. The CHU mentions Var-o in the form of wealth, horses, cattles etc.

Gautama refuses to take wealth etc., but he reminds him to promise, he had given Gautama tells his desire and asks to fulfill it on the basis of firmness in words. then the king specifically mentions that Gautama's desire comes under" divine boon[9] and asks him to have some māṇuṣavara.

The CHU and the BRU both describe the important doctrine of transmigration. It is developed in the Upaniṣadic period. The Rv mentions two paths only but the Rv. does not speak about the period for the enjoyment in the heaven. The Rv. does not speak specifically of the soul's journey. the Brāhmaṇas are more developed and mention that men have to pass through death several times. But even the theory about rebirth based on good or bad deeds is not found also here[11]. The BRU and the CHU mention in clearest words that it is man's own deeds and conduct that lead a men to new births.

P.V. Kane discusses the two paths, he examines Deussen's view, as well as he tries to examine the Ṛgvedic ideas about the two paths. He also evalutes BG's explanation as well as the same in the vedānta. He draws the conclusions in the light of SBH about pañcāgnividyā[12].

It is clear that the CHU and the BRU have the same topic and similar ideas. Now the question arises why both deal with the same points. The Ups. deal with many subjects, some of the common topice like prāṇa, Brahman, jagat, jiva etc. but the manner in which they are handled is different. The passages under study i.e. CHU 5.3.6 and BRU 6.2.4 are handled in the same manner and possibly the reason for its handling in the same manner lies in the fact that the author of the philosophy, but in this Yājñavalkya is to be connected as a student of Āruṇi. It appears that if Yājñavalkya was a pupil of Āruṇi, he must have formed certain concepts in his mind. The Teaching of Āruṇi must have been impressed on him regarding certain topics. and so in the Yājñavalkya's philosophy the effect of the teacher's knowledge is found. The Yājñavalkya put forward the strong basic concepts in the same way as his preceptor revealed them; perhaps Yājñavalkya deals with this subject for expressing his distinct opinion on the subject from his teacher. Deussen's remarks[13] in this connection that "the common source of CHU and

BRU in this section was not a homogenous product, but a welding together of two related sections which however are regarded in a different spirit."

The boon is divided into two categories in the CHU

1. The Daiva (divine) as is of knowledge regarding supreme.

2. Where the mānuṣa (material) boon consists of (a) cow, (b) horse (c) servant (d) clothes (e) gold.

This story stresses that celibacy is one of the requisites for obtaining the knowledge. Gautama became a pupil of the king by utterance. He has not to serve him as a teacher or give him a present. But Max Muller remarks[14] "Gautama actually dwelt as a pupil (of Pravāhaṇa who was a rājanya) in order to obtain the fame of having respectfully served his master." It is to remarked the Max Muller's remark is not endossed by the texts; it presents Āruṇi as a well-known and adorable Brahmin. Pupils came to him for learning. Moreover, the generation of Gautama to which Āruṇi belonged, was supposed to be a learned one, it was famous all over. Max Muller's western thought seems that if Āruṇi having a high status in the society stays with the man having the low status from the caste point of view. does not add dignity to his personality.

Though Pravāhaṇa was from the royal class, inferior than Brahmins, the knowledge which the king had was a supreme one. For securing knowledge Āruṇi's stay at king's place show his curiosity, his inquisitiveness on the other hand. It is not a blame to Āruṇi's personality, but it adds to his modest behaviour. However according to the Max Muller's remark the fame obtained by staying with a king to the Āruṇi will not increase Āruṇi's knowledge. Further Āruṇi never thinks of high or low position or a king in the society. His goal was acquiring knowledge only and he gets it from the king well.

BRU 4.3.1.

A dialogue is recorded in the BRU which took place between the Yājñavalkya and the Janaka. It recasts Yājñavalkya's various views on some of the philosophical matters. The discussion was on the following point viz. The highest light of man: Janaka put a question "what is the light of a man ?" (BRU 4.3.4) and the reply was : the Sun serves as the light for man. It is through the Sun that all actions like sitting, going, breathing are possible. When the sun is not available the moon functions for the same purpose. When the Sun and the Moon both cease to work, the fire and speech work as the light respectively and guide him. Again if all these helping agents are available, it is through the guidance of Ātman that he works or acts. It means Yājñavalkya stresses on the point that the ultimate light of man is Ātman. i.e. to say or is the light within the heart[15].

The Sun, the Moon and the fire etc. are the symbols of light. They have received their lustre from the Supreme light.[16] It is the light which shines above this heaven higher than everything in the highest worlds and it also strengthens Yājñavalkya's principle that the light which is within the man is a unique entity and it is the all pervading one. It illumines the whole universe. Yājñavalkya moves from concrete to abstract[17] thinking in forming' a nature of the soul'. Yājñavalkya explains his thinking about the self with the help of the Sun, the Moon and then goes to abstract thinking i.e. the Ātman. He seeks to harmonise all that is perceptible, with all that is vivid and with all that is subtle. He proceeds step by step from the lowest to the highest. from the worst to the best. It may be said that it leads a journey from darkness to light.

Yājñavalkya elaborates three states corresponding to the three worlds. The states are (1) waking (2) dreaming (3) sleep[18]. The self is present in all the states. It is not illuminated by any outside entity, it is self-illuminated. the soul remains as ever. Its nature does not change in any condition. It does not think or imagine but the self appears to be thinking imagining on account of understanding with its modifications like desire, aversion, pleasure, pain. In the state of liberation the connection with understanding terminates. In the waking condition the soul cognizes all evils, desires, senses and all the rest. The dreaming soul moves along the two states i.e. waking and sleeping, dreaming state is an intermediate state. The soul wanders from one body to another.

He perceives the objects for the time being. Actually in the dreaming state there are no lakes, ponds, birds, animals or any other objects but there he experiences those objects and feels them that they are really existing. He becomes united with such objects and experiences evils or joys, pleasures or pains. The soul imagines different shapes for itself; either laughing with friends. or witnessing terrific sights or someone kills him, some one over powers him, all these are mere imaginings of the soul.

When one goes to deep sleep or when one awakes, all those created objects disappear. Their results also are vanished. The self tries to make the body to sleep but the self remains awake and notices the body to sleep but the self remains awake and notices the impressions of actions that have been left on the mind. He wanders in dream, enjoys a number of things but it creates its own objects of perception and experiences in that state. The soul returns to the place from which he has started to dream. Here Yājñavalkya shows a genuine psychological insight when he states that the soul perceives in dream only that fear which it sees in waking. similarly the soul remains uneffected as specially mentioned by Yājñavalkya and it is one of the main principles of Indian philosophy. At the same time that the self does not require external entity to light, is the basic principle of the Vedānta philosophy.

Yājñavalkya seeks this very idea in a practical but in a suggestive way; e.g. the soul is a bank or boundary. Just as a fish swims along the two banks of a river, so does the soul moves along the two states-sleeping and waking or as a falcon or any bird. Just as having roamed about in the air he becomes tired and descends to its nest, the soul returns from waking to sleeping.

In deep sleep the soul is free from all fancies and vain imaginings, and from the manifold perceptions of waking condition. He is not affected by good or bad effects of the objects. The deep sleep is distinct from unconsciousness. A nice example is cited in this context. Just as a man when in the embrace of his wife knows nothing without or within, so also the soul becomes one with the highest soul in deep state. This state is beyond empirical distinction. The soul possesses no relation, e.g. a father, a son, or a teacher. It throws out the limitations of social laws and regulations but it is turned into simple and pure joy.

In this condition the organs of the body cease to work but the self never loses the function of seeing. Just as fire does not lose the character of burning so long as it is fire, the self sees by its own light.

This is the world of Brahman, the highest goal, the highest bliss.

When one dies the person seperates himself from his gross body even as a fruit seperates itself from its stalk. He goes back to his new abode by the same way he came; there he assumes another form in which he starts to live a new life[19].

The Doctrine of Karma :-

Here Yājñavalkya speaks about the famous doctrine of Indian philosophy i.e. Karma.

The actions of man leads him to the future life. The conduct either good or bad, focusses on the new life. "He becomes pure by pure deeds and sinful by sinful deeds". The performance of a man is a torch to his destiny. Merits and demerits show and guide him a further state of existence. A man carries the puṇyas of his deeds with him after his death. The belief is that an individual is always born with Saṁskāras which are nothing but the thoughts gathered together of the past lives in the abstract forms. The Saṁskāras predominate over the mind, that is why everybody understands the same thing in different manner. The law of Karma holds that every motive in ordinary human life springs from desire and results in impressions which forms the seeds of future activities and desires.

The self is free from good and evil deeds is identical with Brahman and he is the ultimate, the protector of all the world, the self is that out of which all things and all forms of life proceed. The Brahmins try to know him by the study of vedas and by auesterity one who acquires Brahman becomes patient, satisfied and looks upon everything identical with Brahman—of. "Sarvam Khalu idam Brahma". On the other hand one who overcomes from all attachments, becomes free from doubts, is entitled for realisation. This is the fact which Yājñavalkya endevaours to put forward as an ideal before Janaka—the philosopher king. In the words of the MU. it may be said that on knowing which all things are known while the same principle is supported by chu." That by instruction in which the unthought becomes thought and the unknown known." Yājñavalkya's attemps to stress this teaching ends in the identification of Ātman with the Highest self. This is how, Yājñavalkya's philosophy has a kind of practical or ethical end throughout. But here are some points in which his philosophy encompasses strongly than his ethical tendency.

Naturally, at the end of Yājñavalkya's speech Janaka proposed to discard his kingdom and offer himself together with the empire at Yājñavalkya's feet.

BRU 1.3.28

The third section introduces a stroy which emphasises on the superiority of the prāṇa. It is told that two kinds of classes originated from prajāpati (1) Devas and (2) Asuras. Asuras are elders than Devas. Once they were struggling among themselves and trying to overcome these worlds. Gods took help of the sacrifice through Udgītha for conquering demons. Gods requested speech (Vāk) to chant (udgītha) for them. That means whatever enjoyments is in speech it will be obtained for the gods by chanting. When the demons came to know, they rushed and pierced it with evil. Futher nose, eye, ear mind were requested to chant in the sacrifice for gods respectively. All the organs failed in chanting the udgītha as they were destroyed with evil. At last they went to vital breath and proposed it to chant for them. Demons desired to pierce the vital breath but their efforts proved in vail. Demons were scattered in all directions, and they perished, therefore, the vital prāṇa is regarded to be supreme one. This deity carried them beyond death. This vital breath is compared with sāman because it is equal to (sāma) or the universe. This is also called as Udgītha for it upholds the universe. The person is well acquainted with the tone (wealth) obtains wealth. Naturally the priest must possess a rich tone in his voice while performing the duties of a ṛtvija. He must know the correct sound of a mantra, in order to produce the desired fruit either for himself or for the sacrificer.

It is said that when the prastotr priest recites the chant, the sacrificer must recite the following lines when he begins to sing the sāman :

> *"Lead me from the unreal to the real,*
> *Lead me from darkness to light;*
> *Lead me from death to immortality."*[20]

"It is only when he chants the prayer in this strain that he is able to transcend the regions of darkness and death."[21]

By this prayer the sacrificer wishes to be immortal. By chanting the other prayers in the hymns of praise, one should secure food by chanting. And therefore he should wish to fulfill his desired object in them; whether it may choose for himself or other. the fruit of chanting properly laid by the inscriptions is world conquering as Radhakrishnan remarks "because the performer reaches the divinity he worship."[22]

It is such a kind of boon where the desired fruit becomes the boon. On the part of a person. The way of praising secures the fulfillment. " he should choose a boon whatever desire he may have." The word "Boon" is used in sense of "fruit". In the above mentioned boon, there are not two interlocuters as compared to other stories under study; or no sort of communications. Generally a grantee wished a reward from a granter. While here a particular mode of recitation prescribed by scriptures includes a boon or choice on the part of chanter. It is connected with ritualism on one hand and with cosmology on the other. S.K Belvalkar remarks[23] "Thus the cosmological result arrives that speech and breath, eye, ear and mind in the microcosm were able to produce Agni, Vāyu, Āditya, space and Moon in the macrocosm."

The passage undertaken implies that there is an act or process which leads to immortality. It postulates a fundamental aspiration of man. This aspiration is threefold Viz. leading from unreal to the real, from darkness to light, etc. Here darkness and the unreal are death and immortality is light and that is real. Thus the passage starts from metam psychosis and ends in metaphysic. " light" is nothing but the self that to know that there is a light within when this light shines all other things perishes.

KATU

Naciketas secured three boons from Yama, the god of death when Yama came to know that the Brahmin boy remained on fasting for three nights Yama showed respect to him instead of subjecting him to his rule. Yama was not present when Naciketas went to his abode. It is father's curse made Naciketas to go to Yama's place. Naciketas' father, viz. Vājaśravas, cursed him when he spent all his wealth to the Brahmins as a sacrificial gift of the Viśvajit sacrifice. Naciketa's father was offering weak and steril cows as gifts. When Naciketas realised that the gift of such old and lean cows would result into sinful deeds; the boy went to his father and asked, "To whom will you give me? "(KATU 1.1.4) The father did not listen to the boy's question and remained silent. But Naciketas' frequent questions made him angry and so he cursed him that he was given to death. thus the father's command and the desire for keeping the truth, and righteousness compelled Naciketā to go to Yama's residence. Yama felt guilty because of his own absence in the house and in order to remove the evil effects of keeping a Brahmin hungry, Yama decided to please him with three boons. Yama bestowed three boons, on Naciketas two of them were material i.e. on the lower levels; and the third one was spiritual i.e. on the higher level. By the first boon Naciketas had the appeased anger and composed mind of his father when he returned to his home. Yama accepted his first request and replied that Naciketas' father would behave with love as before and would forget his anger. The first boon i.e. "peace of mind for his father" reveals Naciketas' soft and kind nature of a human being.

The second boon was about the knowlegde of the way rendering one's good works imperishable. He sought to have peep into the heaven. In the earlier times the popular belief was that the sacrifice lead to heaven which was considered as safe and delightful. There in no fear, all rejoice in heaven was also believed. The idea of heaven might have arisen. Out of desire to go beyond the physical world and life. Yama readily grants Naciketas' second wish and explains him the fire-sacrifice which leads to heaven. Yama offers an extra boon to him that the sacrifice will be known by his name.

This addition of one boon is fore runner of the Purāṇic feature, viz. offering of rewards more than asked for. Here also Yama told the fruit of Naciketa-fire i.e. the person who performs this sacrifice by giving alms etc. will overcome the realm of repeatition of birth. Moreover he will attain supreme peace.

Yama now proceeds on the fulfillment of a third boon. Naciketas desired to instruct him on the topic viz. whether the soul exists or it does not exists after death. The question of Naciketas relates to the truth of life. More over this gives rise to other questions like:—Is there anything abiding in life or in the world ? which principle rules over life ? Yama-Naciketas in this dialogue brings an interesting feature of boon as in the Purāṇa. Yama is here a god; while Naciketas is a mortal but a youth. It is not the old that inquires the possibility of life afte death; but it is a kumāra that puts a question in the KATU. Usually the old man puts such questions, while the story shows Naciketas a young boy who is a matured one.

With reference to the last enquiry of Naciketas Yama tried to dissadue him by arguing that it is not easy to understand it; it is not only difficult to know but also subtle in nature.[25]

Yama asked him to choose another boon and requested

him to make free Yama from his promise. Yama is not willing to disclose the mystery, he is evasive in replying and also a great temptor; where as in other ups. The teacher answers the questions put to him by his pupils/seekers and he is not evasive. Yama hesitated to grant his last boon and tempted him by putting various other alternatives, which would attract the body's mind. He asked to have sons, a life of hundred years, herds of cattle, horses, gold wealth, rulership over earth, other pleasures difficult to get in the mortal world and musical instruments etc. This attitude of Yama may suggest that he wanted to test him if he is or not ordinary and immature. Perhaps Yama might be thinking that the philosophy of Ātman is propounded to such a unworthy boy, he will make no use of it and that it will be a futile and insensible act on the part of Yama. But the story shows Yama's discriminating mind and one pointed determination.

All the alternatives placed before Naciketas did not move him an inch. Though Naciketas was young in age, he was intellectually firm and mature. The boy was not satisfied with such empty and short-lived pleasures. He refused to accept them and forced the god of death to disclose that this wisdom which gives the everlasting bliss and not the momentary one. Naciketas rejected all the temptations on the ground that they gave rise to endless urge.

Naciketas stands firmly on his original request and he also told that now it was upto Yama to keep his promise or not. This answer of him makes Yama pleased when the boy established his fitness to grasp and receive the benefit of the knowledge of the truth; so Yama started to instruct him. First of all Yama refers to two aspects viz. (1) Śreyas and (2) preyas. Both of them take hold of man. The term "Śreyas" means which is good, which leads to true welfare, which is ultimately beneficial. While "preyas" contains happiness which arises from organic satisfaction, if a man considers this as the be-all and end-all of life, his life will be lived at a very lowlevel.

While "Śreyas" involves two levels-The dharma and amrta. The good life and the divine life-immortal life. The good life is not an ultimate; not an end in itself, it must leaf to the realisation of the Ātman, the true self of man.[27] "Śreyas" and "preyas" and free choice. "Śreyas" leads to life of wisdom, while "preyas" leads to life of ignorance. The wise prefers "Śreyas" to "preyas" but the ordinary person chooses preyas-through the love of gain and attachment. It tries to capture his attention and interest. "preyas" conduces immediate profit and pleasure but its inside is hollow; while "Śreyas" is spiritual illumination. Most of the men are not aware of it. Ātman is beyond logical reasoning. To comprehend it will is difficult and wonderful also. The Up. emphasises the uniqueness of the knowledge relating to Ātman. It is the product of vision and not of intellectual cleverness. It is not easy to understand. It is difficult to be seen and is very subtle. It resides within the body. In every act of knowledge viz. perception and judgement Ātman is present. It is beyond the cause and effect, virtue and vice; time and space.

The self is unborn, eternal immutable and everlasting. It is not slain, when the body is destroyed. It is not killed by one or it is not responsible for killing. The self is the smaller than the atom and greater than the cosmos. One who is free from desire and grief knows the glory of it. The iśu[28] speaks about the same idea.

All the vedas declare the syllable 'om' as supreme whosoever knows this sound, his desires are accomplished in Infinite. 'om' is Brahman. Yama praises the glory of this divine symbol.[29] The earnest words of Sanatkumāra in CHU[30] also explains the same thought that the Infinite alone is happiness.

Further Yama compares the universal soul and Individual soul with shade and light as set forth in the simile of the two birds in MU.[31] The universal soul abides together with it, regulates its actions and witnesses its experiences. Brahman is the light of all light and jīva is its reflection, it moves towards fulfilment from body to body, while Brahman is free from such movements.

Further Yama proceeds to compare the body with a chariot. Buddhi as a charioteer, manas as veins and the Ātma as the ruler of it. just as a chariot gets its motive power from the horses yoked to it, similarly the body gets it motive from the sense organs, consisting of the nervous system and the brain. He who is devoid of correct understanding his senses become uncontrolled like the bad horses of a charioteer. But who is possessed of right understanding, his senses become controlled like the good horses of a charioteer. He reaches the goal from where there is no return. The self is greater than the buddhi, manas, sense-organs and sense-objects respectively.

The self is not manifested though it is omnipresent. It is not the object but the subject to knower. It does not reveal as such to one and all ordinary people, as well as great scholars fail to comprehend. It because it is hidden and subtler. Similarly Ātman is not unknown. It can be seen, it can be realised. Awakening of man's mind is required to reach this inborn divinity. this peculiar thought is expressed again and again in KATU[32] (2.3.14.). When a man succeeds in controlling sense organs, and the mind; something wonderful happens. It brings him the mystery of his own self before him present. One becomes free from the jaws of death when he realises the self as soundless, touchless, formless without smell, without taste immutable, imperishable. This is the underlying principle of the universe. This self manifests itself in various forms of the nature like air, fire etc. It is only one principle. It is not exhausted in any one of its manifestations. it assumes various forms, having entered the world according to the different objects: The lightening agents like sun, moon, stars which give light to the world, do not shine when he shines. The self is the ultimate light of all, everything shines after it.

Yama explains his teaching with an illustration of Aśvattha tree as Brahman, e.g. the tree having its root above and branches below. Brahman is the root-cause of this universe. He resides in the highest place and the branches are visible in this created world. That root principle, that origin of the creation is to be searched off. The Up. always emphasises on the union with Brahman as the Highest goal. It is the aim of life for accomplishing this end the Ups. ask us to undergo a strict discipline of cleanliness, fasting continence and solitude. passion is to be checked and compassion, kindness, love for living creatures should be observed.

Meditation and concentration are also requisite in order to realise the oneness with Brahman. KATU says: (2.6.15) when all ties are serened immortality is achieved, here on the earth. i.e. (sā kāṣṭhā sā parā gati). This is the highest supreme goal. The self is not realised by mere talk or by mere knowledge. It is attained by the man who thirsts for it with his whole heart and soul, with his keen desire to know him. To such a person alone the self reveals its real nature. Yama speaks: "the self is not known by knowledge nor by mind, nor by hearing discourses. It reveals itself to the one whom it chooses as his own. (KATU 1.2.23). The instruction of Yama to Naciketas involves the doctrine of grace.

Comments on KATU

The KATU discusses the concept or nature of soul. Naciketas third boon was about the 'soul' i.e. what happens to the soul when one passes away. That means the soul is expected to take it as the Highest soul. When the thought of the Highest Soul persists it relates to the other world. That means the soul is expected to take it as the Highest soul. When the thought of the Highest soul persists it relates to the other world. It concerns about the next world; so naturally Yama with draws Naciketas mind from choosing that boon which implies the existence of a soul; which is considered as a difficult problem, which is difficult to grasp also. The KATU touches the philosophy of a soul which is not easy to understand.

The KATU mentions two means i.e. Śreyas and preyas for attaining the highest soul. compare CHU 5.3.10. and BRU 6.2.5 ft. as well as KAU 1.1; The KATU discusses the same problem but as these ups. state the paths i.e. Devayāna and pitṛyāna fully; what happens when the soul passes, by which form he is transformed into this world e.g. Rain, cereal, food, semen respectively.

The KATU does not touch it in its full form. Now the question arises: when a person passes away the soul becomes free, but it is not the case that soul obtains salvation immediately; still the soul is liberated; he must have gone through various stages. There must be a transmigration-stage of the soul.

How does the soul ascend up ? The KATU does not touch this problem. Just it mentions the two different ways and states that generally persons choose "preyas-mārga" and not the Śreyas-one. Moreover it seems that when Naciketas prefers "Śreyas" Yama becomes happy. He remarks that those who prefers "preyas" they become the subject of senses; they enjoy various pleasures and delights, grief and unhappiness in this world. They are bound to be born again and again. On the other hand those who wish to go by

"Śreyas-mārga," they are entitled to have emancipation, because the path ultimately leads to salvation. No doubt "Śreyas" is difficult to follow. The Ātman is described in a chariot imaginary; as well as the root cause of the world, like a aśvattha tree of which the root is hidden in up and the branches are downward seen clearly in this world. The source of the universe is described as aṅgusthamātra, stays in pura etc.

Thus the KATU deals with one of the major aspect about, the soul but the Up. leaves the other part of it; what happens to the soul in the next world. about this point the KATU does not throw light anywhere. Similarly for the other way i.e. preyas . The KATU remains silent. The Up. does not touch this part of this question.

The Varāha Purāṇa (chapter 193 to 212) also deals with the same story. Here the characters e.g. Naciketas and Yama are present but they do not discuss philosophy. The atmosphere and the situation are different. Moreover there is a full-fleched description of the soul when he passes on to the Yama-loka. The type of miseries and grief he experiences, is stated in details, but here the context is distinct. Naciketas returns to his father from Yama's abode and than ṛṣis asked him what he had seen there; and what he had experienced there. Naciketas gives all information i.e. how Yamaloka is, the miseries in Naraka, the punishments delights etc. if a man commits particular sin, a particular reward is meant for it.

KAU 1.1

The conversation between the king citra-Gārgyāaṇī[33] and Śvetaketu consists of jaivali's speculations on the eschatology again with few variations as compared to those in the CHU and BRU. The dialogue points out Śvetaketu's failure to reply to king's query. When the king asked him, where he would place the king; which is the hidden place[34] Śvetaketu was sent to king Gārgyāyani's sacrifice as a chief priest by his father—Āruṇi, instead of himself on the request of the king. The father's command forced Śvetaketu to approach the king. Śvetaketu belonged to a learned family. He was taught by his father who is presented as a knower of Brahman, and an honourable Brahmin. But Śvetaketu appears as ignorant because he replies that he does not know. In BRU and CHU he presents the same picture of himself. Now the question that comes up, is why Śvetaketu gives such a negative reply. Does he really know or does not know or perhaps he wants to hide something. Another question that arises is that whether the king really possesses such knowledge. The answer to this question is that the king does possess this knowledge, because it is he who imparts this knowledge to Śvetaketu. It can be concluded that Āruṇi wanted to remove Śvetaketu's pride as the Ups. presents him as a very proud character. The Up. does not mention the reason at all, as to why such a question was put to him. The question proposed by citra was about the transmigration of a soul, the secret place where soul approaches when it departs. It also concerns about the paty by which it ascends to the higher world.

Śvetaketu returned home and asked about the reply to his father. Āruṇi came to understand that there remained something more to be learnt. So along with his son taking sacrificial twings in his hand[35] he went to the king's assembly and told the king "I am present".[36]

Whle observing Āruṇi's prideless behaviour citra honoured him with customary rites and asked the reason about his presence in the king's assembly. Gautama told him that he wanted to know the answers of the questions which the king put forth to his son. The king readily accepted his request and explained the vidyā.

Citra explains the soul's journey after death. All the souls go to the Moon, when they depart from this world. The Moon is the door of heaven. from this place the soul ascends up or descends down. In the region of Moon knowledge obtained by the soul is tested. if the soul in question does not have the required knowledge the Moon throws it down to the world. If the Moon is satisfied it goes to the heaven. The distinction can be sharply drawn in the KAU from BRU and CHU. The order of the descent of the soul is in the following order-rain, cereals. the womb of the woman respectively. It lives on the earth, learns to distinguish truth and untruth. If he realises that he is no other entity distinct from the supreme soul, he goes up and becomes one with the world of Brahmā.

The soul after death, proceeds by the path of Devayāna to the world of Fire, to world of air, to the world of water, to the world of Indra, to the world of prajāpati, and lastly to the world of Brahmā [37]. The modern scientist viz. George Meek tries to prove with the modern equipments that the soul does not die when the body dies. A person undergoes a transformation and assumes a new a fresh body in the other world according to Meek's view. Similarly he tells that as a person goes up the piece of cloth rolled round the soul's body shines more and more. The cloth in this context does not mean physical cloth, it has astral structure, astral touch in a way.

Citra-Gārgyāyani describes the heavenly world as semi-mythical and semiphilosophical as constrasted with the world of man. The world of Brahmā has a lake called āra.[38]

The world possesses the river "Virajā" (devoid of age), the tree Illyah[39] the city bounded by all sides by sāla trees; [40] The palace aparājitam; two doorkeepers Indra and Prajāpati; the Brahman's hall viz vibhu, His throne vicakṣaṇā (intelligence)[41], the couch (paryaṅka) of incomparable splendour and the manasi (imaginary), the nymphs Ambāḥ (Sruti-sacred scriptures) and the Ambayavi (buddhi-understanding), the river Ambayā (the undecaying and the streams that lead to the knowledge of Brahman). Brahman receives the liberated soul. Further the king fully describes how the soul is welcomed by nymphs with the fruits, powders, clothes, perfumes, garlands, ornaments worthy of Brahman. The knower of Brahman moves to lake āra, crosses it by his mind. while those, who come without knowing Brahman, are drowned. The moment called Yeṣṭihā flee from him. He comes to the river Virajā and crosses it by his mind and there he discards good and bad deeds. His dear relatives get his good actions, while his enemies get his evil actions.

The frame of mind is illustrated by a nice simile, i.e. just as one driving in a chariot looks down the two wheels (without being touched by them) in the same way the soul who has acquired the Brahman remains untouched.

When he approaches the Illyaḥ tree the Brahmic odour enters into him, when he comes to the city sālajya, Brahmic flavour enters into him, when he approaches the palace-aparājitā; the splendour of Brahman reaches him; and when he approaches the hall-vibhu, the Brahmic glory enters into him. He comes to the throne of Intelligence.

The throne (paryaṅka) is a couch having four feet. The KAU describes the "couch" metaphorically. The sāman-verses Bṛhad and Rathantara are the eastern feet of the throne. The Sāman verses shaita and Naudhasa are its western feet. The Sāmans Vairūpa and Vairāja are its sides length-wise. The Sāmans Sakvara and Raivat are the east and west sides. This throne is knowledge. with the help of the self-knowledge he sees clearly. He reaches the couch of incomparable splendour.

It is prāṇa (vital air). The past and future are its eastern feet. The Sāmans Bṛhad and Raṭhantara are the two sides lengthwise. The Sāmans Bhadra and Yajñā-Yajñīnya are its two cross sides at the head and feet; the ṛc and Sāman are the long sheets, the Yajus, the cross sheets; the moon beams are the cushion, the Udgītha is the coverlet and the fortune is the pillow.

This description of couch looks new in the Ups. but it is not invented by KAU. Since we learn similar type of description in the earlier authority viz. AB 8.3. AB 8.3 describes the coronation ceremony of Indra. That may be compared with the description of couch. It is told in AB that the seat or throne for Indra is prepared from the wood of Udumbara tree. that seat is called Ṛc of which the Bṛhat and Rathantara Sāmans are its front feet and Vairupa and Vairāja are its back feet etc. the ṛg, yajus mantras are its weaves etc. Thus AB 8.3 serves as prototype idea for KAU.

Like the KAU, the CHU and the BRU also describe the two different paths at the end of pañcāgnividyā with a slight difference. In them the paths are called Devayāna and pitṛyāna, sometimes the rights and left or the southern or northern. The soul travels from light and day to the bright half of the Moon, in the Devayāna and in the pitṛyāna, it passes from smoke and night to the dark half of the Moon.

Both the roads meet at Moon and diverge afterwards. The main difference between the two paths is that those who travel on the former path do not return again on the earth but reach in the end, a true knowledge of Brahman; while those who pass on by the pitṛyāna, become the subject of rebirth. The spiritual persons are always prepared to accept truth of life; they always go higher and higher.

Radhakrisan[42] holds the view that all the departed souls reach the Moon by the way of fathers; but it is to be observed that the KAU does not refer to any specific path for asceding the soul after death. The MU[43] also describes that a performer of sacrifice goes to the place of Lord i.e. if the sacrificer offers oblations at the proper time the flames viz. rays of the Sun lead to him in the meritorious world to Brahman, where he gets respect by pleasant speech. Similarly the KAU also states that a liberated soul attains the Brahmā-loka where he is welcomed by hundreds of nymphs and he is honoured well.

The KAU explains that the person who has done good deeds follows the path of gods and merges into Brahmā. He becomes free from the realm of rebirth. Here again the KAU fist describes a path and then paryaṅkavidyā, while in the CHU and the BRU[44], the pañcāgnividyā is told at first and then the knower of vidyā goes by this path etc. that is why here a question may arise: does it mean that the paryaṅka vidyā is superior to the pañcāgnividyā? It may be said that both the Ups. viz. CHU and KAU deal with the same question some how or other, both of them try to solve the problem. The Upaniṣatkāra knew that the soul did not merge into Brahman immediately after its death. Therefore there might be some stages when the man passes away, till he unites with Brahman. Thus there is no question of superiority or of inferiority between the pañcāgnividyā and paryaṅka vidyā. But it may be said that the Kauṣitaki upaniṣatkāra put forth more advanced thought while dealing and describing the Devayāna mārga and how the soul passes through various world viz. it goes to the Moon. Fire, Air, Vāyu, Indra and Prajāpati respectively. On the other hand CHU is earlier than KAU, the CHU did not describe Devayāna in details. The CHU only tells whosoever goes by Devayāna, becomes Brahman. And the said Up. is silent about the intermediate stages, when the soul ascends up. And the development in thoughts is clearly seen at the time of KAU1.1.

Secondly, in the CHU and the BRU and the KAU, the person viz. Śvetaketu's father viz. Āruṇi Gautama, who attains the knowledge remain the same. In the CHU an the BRU Gautama goes to the king Jaivali but in the KAU both Śvetaketu and Gautama went to the king citra. In all the three Ups. Śvetaketu's reply remains same viz. "he did not know the the answer". In the light of the comparision of this with the one in the KAU; Gautama though a learned Brahmin is depicted as ignorant of paryaṅkavidyā.

Gautama is shown inquisitive for the secret knowledge in the CHU, the BRU and the KAU. The granter of the boon belongs to the Kṣatriya class, is Jaivali in the CHU and the BRU. Though a Kṣatriya stood on a lower level in the varṇa hierarchy, but he possessed knowledge which a Brahmin did not.

The BG[45] also speaks about the two paths as Śukla-kṛṣṇa gati. The BG stresses the philosophical facts of the up. It remains faithful to the upaniṣadic teaching of the two paths which lead the soul, after death. The person gets salvation; he acquires "paramaṁ dhāma"[46] as the BG describes.

KAU 3.1.

The third adhyāya of the KAU presents a new doctrine within a story. Indra, a god, is personified as a human being. He is the granter of a boon and pratardana the king of Kāśī, the son of Divodāsa is a grantee. He reached the abode of Indra through fighting and efforts. Indra was pleased with him and asked Pratardana to fulfil his desire. pratardana never expressed to have spiritual or material objects directly as compared to Āruṇi and Janaka vide : (in the CHU 5.3.6 in the BRU 4.3.1 respectively). Pratardana left the choice of the desired object to Indra, the god of war himself to be granted. But he specified then what soever of as a boon which would be most beneficial to mankind. Indra refused to do so on the basis of an arguement viz. "A superior won't choose for the inferior (KAU 3.1)".

As pratardana was not ready to hold Indra's point, he became ready to go back without a boon remarking that "he did not want a boon (KAU 3.2)". Indra was bound by this word. To keep the promise was indra's duty, and this compelled him to satisfy recipient's request. Indra granted the boon to pratardana according to his desire. Thus the dialogue brings out that the boon may be selected and granted by the superior to the junior even if a small conditioning is specified; and it is not obligatory to a grantee to select a boon. Usually one who grants the boon is on a higher level, but he maintains the freedom of the recipient.

Indra offered him the doctrine of life-breath. He identifies prāṇa and prajñātman with himself. He teaches the Brahmavidyā considering it as the most wholesome for man, viz. "Know me" (KAU 3.2.) This means that the KAU suggests Indra's knowledge is most beneficient. Indra is the truth. and he also preaches that understands him only.

The knowledge of Indra is so effective, that even if a person has commitedsins like mātṛ-pitṛ vadha bhṛuṇahatyā, stealing. it destroys the bad results of these sins. It means a person never remains a human being but he gives up his manhood and becomes one with Indra. i.e. to say when ātmajñāna is obtained the person never experiences the fruits of Karmans. This suggests that the up does not accept here the doctrine of karman. The bad deeds are enumerated but the Up. is not clear whether the person has to experience the reward of good or bad deeds. The Brahmajñāna reduces all karman to zero according to the KAU 3.1 and the Brahmajñāna is equivalent to the mokṣa.

Indra compares himself with the life-breath (Prāṇa) and advises pratardana to meditate on him as intelligent self, as life as immortality. The sense organs and objects are internally related to each other. They live together in the body. there is life till the breath holds in the body. Both of them leave the body at the same time. "They originate as two stems of different kinds.[47]" The breathing spirit alone controls the body and leads to proper action. The dumb, the deaf, the lame etc. are seen without sense organs but the life breath resides in them. The breathing spirit is the intelligent self and vice-versa. When the person is asleep, he is united with that breathing spirit alone. All the organs of the body reside there in sound sleep. when he awakes, the vital breath reaches to their respective organs as the sparks proceed from a blazing fire into all directions. when a man is about to die, he is incapable of hearing, thinking speaking etc. The individual soul becomes one in that breathing spirit; then all sensations go to it and when it gives up the body, they all depart from the body.

All the senses viz. speech, perception, smell, taste are the parts of intelligence. The perceived objects are external but the act of perception is internal. It is through intelligence. There is cognition and it remains effective. Without consciousness the knowledge is impossible.

Without its support all the perceptive and active senses along with speech and are powerless and incapable of grasping their objects. "My mind was absent." says the man, And therefore I did not perceive the object (KAU 3.7). Thus it is only when consciousness stays, that man can cognise all names by speech, all forms by the eye, hear all sounds by the ear and think all thoughts by the mind.[48]

The Up. goes further to point out as follows:— Try to find out the speaker and not what speech is, the smeller and not what smell is, the hearer, the food-eater etc. The odour, speech, form, sound, deed, delight, pains are not the objects to be desired, to understand but one should know them as external elements with reference to the intelligence. These are further related to the objects of existence that is they are dependent on each other. If there are no objects, there would be no subjects; and if there are no subjects, there woukd be no objects. Thus anything can be known with both the sides. One side proves incompleteness. The existent elements are held by elements of knowing which are fixed in prāṇa. The illustration is cited by the KAU 3.8.e.g. The felly of a wheel is held by the spokes which are themselves fixed in the nave. So also the elements of existence are fixed in the elements of intelligence; and further they are fixed in the breathing spirit. This very breathing spirit, the consciousness, is bliss; it is ageless and immortal. The knower of it does not becomes great or small by good or evil action. This spirit causes a man to perform good actions woim he wants to lead up from these worlds, and also he is the cause of bad action of a person whom he wishes to throw down. This peculiar thought expressed by the KAU comes nearer to Vallabhācārya's doctrine of grace.

Hereto Indra identifies this prāṇa with the conscious self or prajñātman; and again prajñātman with himself. This prajñātman is inspirer of all actions; the protector, the ruling principle, the lord of all. He is sovereignity of the world. "He is my self," "This one should understand." (KAU 3.8).

Indra personifies himself as an almighty, the supreme one. One should adore him as the highest self, the Ātman. This provides the result of immortality on the part of a worshipper.

MAU 1.2 (Maitrāyani Upaniṣad)

The first Chapter introduces the king Bṛhadraṭha and a sage Śākāyanya with unusual trend in the upaniṣadic literature. The story relates that the king discards worldly pleasures and delights, goes to the forest to practise severe penance. He becomes indifferent towards worldly objects, because they are transitory. Having placed his son on the throne the king performed very hard auesterity, viz. He stood in opposite direction, constantly looked at the Sun. After a number of days a sage called Śākāyanya, who was the knower of self, and lustrous like a blazing fire, came there. Śākāyanya was pleased with the ling, so he asked Bṛhadraṭha to fulfil his wish. The king requested to instruct him about the secret of the self. Śākāyanya tempted him to prefer any other request instead of it on the ground that the king's question was difficult to answer. It is instructive to compare here the behaviour of Yama when he tried to withdraw Naciketas' mind from the question about the life after death. The king Bṛhadraṭha fell down at the feet of the sage and begged to tell him the knowledge of the self. The king's reply shows his non-attachment. He argues as follows:—"What is the good of the enjoyment of desires for this body which is unsubstantial, made of bone, skin, muscles, flesh, blood, tears etc. this body is afflicted with desires, anger, delusion, fear, despair, envy, thirst old-age, disease, sorrow etc." (MAU 1.3) We notice that all being perish ultimately, the gnats, mosquitoes, grass and trees grow and decay. The mighty worriors, great kings and emperors have to pass away from this earth. Even the greatest ocean dries up and mountains crumble the fixed stars fall down." (MAU. 1.4). The king wanted to know the principle which remains steadfast, undestructible. His idea is that everything in the world rises and grows, decays and dies finally.

It is on accont of the destructible nature of the existence that the king insists upon having self's knowledge which is everlasting. Again and again the king requests to make him free from the changing world as he was rotted like a frog in a waterless well (MAU-1.4). This utterance of the king moved the sage to teach him the secret principle.

It is to be observed here that in the stories discussed so far the grantee of a boon is not supposed to be worthy of having more knowledge. Moreover the receiver never points out what is known and what is unknown. (cf. MAU 1.2.3). i.e. The king Bṛhadraṭha describes the perishabke nature of the world. He is aware of that there must be some principle which is immutable, everlasting, Therefore he stresses to tell about that principle to the granter of the boon viz. Śākāyanya. On the contrary in the other stories like BRU 4.3.1. ft; KATU, the granter of a boon tells how the world is transitory, and only the knowledge about the ruling principle leads to immortality. But here is a case, where the receiver speaks on the nature of the world, body etc. He is perfectly aware of what remains to be added to his knowledge. The king is highly mature and discriminative, he therefore requested Śākāyanya to impart him that particular knowledge only. Similarly it can be remarked that the character of the king Bṛhadraṭha differs from those of Jaivali, and Citra-Gārgyāyaṇi who surpass Brahmins in the field of jñāna. That is to say the story undertaken shows the king Bṛhadraṭha, from a Kṣatriya class, though highly discriminative, is devoid of superior knowledge. Thus this tends to suggest that all the kings did not possess the secret knowledge; but some secret was hidden from them.

Having taken into account the capacity and capability of attaining his purpose and will, the sage became ready to explain the Brahmavidyā which was delivered to him by Maitri, and to the Vālakhilyās by Prajāpati-Kratu. Śākāyanya imparts -"this indeed is thy self." (MAU 2.3). The self is described as responsible for the motion of the body and he makes the body intelligent. He is pure, holy, clean, tranquil, independent and eternal. He is unborn and undecaying. He remains aloof among all the qualities.

He is subtle, ungraspable, invisible one. He is declared to dwell in the body without any previous awareness, as the man who is in fast asleep; awakes of his own awareness. That part of him which is entirely intelligent in every person is the spirit the self. The self proceeds upwards from the gross body to the subtle body. It is unmodified, unmoved though apparantly it appears as modified due to impressions and wandering in various ways. "That supremely tranquil self, rising out of this body, attains to the supreme light and appears in his own form."[49]

In the beginning prajāpati the lord of creatures was alone. He felt unhappy because of his loneliness. Number of off-springs were born out of him when he meditated on himself. Again all of them were without life, without motion and without intelligence like a stone. He thought of entering inside of them in order to inspire them, make them alive. He assumed the form of air and try to enter into but he failed to do so. He divided himself into fivefold and is called five prāṇas i.e. prāṇa, Apāna, Samāna, Udāna and Vyāna. That breath which rises up is prāṇa, while Apāna is that which moves down: that by which these two are supported is the Vyāna. The Samāna is the breath that distributes subtle material into each limb and carries to the Apāna, the gross food. It is a higher form of the Vyāna and between them the Udāna is produced-that which brings up and carries down what has been eaten or drunk. "Between prāṇa Apāna" the self-resplendent one created heat, this heat is the puruṣa and puruṣa is the fire within man which digests the food that is eaten.[55] (MAU 2.6) Prajāpati did not feel even then happy. So he thought of enjoying the objects. By means of perceptive organs he enjoyed. A common comparison of chariot and the body is given. The body constitutes a chariot, the mind as charioteer, the perceptive organs are reins, while the organs of actions are horses of it. The whip is made of one's character. The body moves round and moves like a wheel (driven by) a potter. Thus the body possesses intelligence by the self which is controlled by it. (MAU 2.6).

This Up. also discusses the individual self which is affected by fruits of actions, pairs of opposites. This self is composed of gross and subtle elements. It is likely to be the subject of nature's qualities easily. On account of confusion this individual soul did not experience the 'self' who dwells in himself. This bhūtātman is unstable; it is wavering, and full of passion and lust. He falsely thinks that he is the doer and this is mine. (MAU-3.2) It is made of bones, flesh, bile, phlegmerror etc. It is a combination of (1) Tāmasa (2) Rājasa qualities. viz. (1) Fear, sleep, age, hurt, hunger, grief, jealousy, changability (2) Affection, passion, injury, restlessness activity, rivalry, instability respectively. It achieves many forms because of these qualities. "Bhūtātman forms the second approach to the problem of Reality."[51]

The discussion of self and soul implies their unity but the question is how they are united. This point is considered by providing many other natural examples which are existent, visible in this world. i.e. like the waves in large rivers; tthere is no turning back of them.

The identification of one's own nature results into freedom from all bondages, performances of the duties lies with the person during the stages of life. Practice of penance is supposed as a chief necessity for gaining knowledge; the arguement that only the performance of penance makes one free from duties is improper, because auesterity results into perfection gradually. "Goodness is obtained by auesterity and from goodness understanding is reached and from understanding the self is obtained. And one who obtains self does not return." (MAU 4.3).

Brahman is realised through knowledge, penance, and meditation. One experiences Brahman when he contemplates on 'AUM'. That leads to unmeasurable happiness. AUM is equal to Praṇava, Udgītha. The MNU[52] also describes 'OM' as the symbol of Brahman. The MAU might have borrowed 'OM' philosophy from the MNU. AUM is formless, it is light. It is divides into threefold. i.e. AUM consists of three letters viz. a, u, m. By means of these, all this world is woven, warp and wool across him. AUM is called as Praṇava. By continuous worship of this holy syllable one secures what he wants."[53] says the Ups.

The gods like Brahmā, Viṣṇu, Rudra, and the natural phenomena like fire, air, sun, are differnt from Brahman but they are the chief forms of the "Immortal one". One meditates on various forms of the Lord. these forms show the proceeding path and then one gets unity with 'Self' into which the universe is merged.

The main purpose of the Up. is to emphasise on the point that there is only one Supreme Self which is to be hankered and that various forms are nothing but the manifestations of that oneself. Spiritual knowledge can be acquired by many modes of worships like contemplating on AUM; with mystic utterances like Bhūr, Bhūvaḥ; Svar or with the Sāvitri prayer.

The MAU deals with the various topics and problems concerning with philosophy; therefore the following remarks of R.D. Ranade[54] seems to be observed in the case of the MAU. "The truth is that in the case of Upaniṣadic philosophers it does not generally rain, but when it does rain, it pours profusely." "Very often the philosophers are pertient, they never illuminate on any topic except the one which is immediately before them and according to the capacity of the learner." As compared to MAU, it deals and discusses almost all the topics relating to philosophy. The king asked to impart the knowledge of Brahman. No further querry by a king is put forth; viz. how it can be obtained etc.

RU. (Rāmottara-Tāpini Upaniṣad)

The dialogue between Yājñavalkya and Atri deals with the exposition of the unqualified Brahman for the benefit of seekers after liberation.

Once a great sage Yājñavalkya won in a contest in the capital of the royal sage Janaka. He lived with a number of disciples. Yājñavalkya taught that those who have middle qualifications, would attain salvation through the worship of Tāraka-mantra of Śri-Rāma in Avimukta. The story of how Śri-Rāma bestowed upon the lord Śiva is narrated. In this contest Śiva is said worshipped him by japa, homa and arcanā. Śiva requested him to grant a boon for the worshipper that if a person died either at the Manikarṇika ghāt or else where on the banks of Ganges in the sacred city, viz. Avimukta, he/she would be released. Being plesased with Śiva Śri-Rāma fulfilled Śiva's uttermost desire and promised him to liberate the person who died on the banks of the Ganges at Kāśi and also that the liberated person would reach Him also whether the dying one might be a worm, an insect or of any other category and also that He himself would be present in stones, idols and like in a hallowed form and also that the person who worships Śri-Rāma with true devotion uttering the Tāraka mantra in that sacred spot would be freed from all sins like Brahminicide, stealing gold, etc.

The Tāraka Up. explains 'Om' sound as Tāraka i.e. deliverer. It distinguishes six elements in it. (a, u, m half-morae bindu and nāda). The terms Nāda and Bindu are well-known in the tantrik texts, and in Indian vernaculars.

Nāda is produced from the inter-action of Bindu and Nāda contains the indistinct sounds of all the letters of the alphabet,[55], Nāda is multiple, it is a product. Every animal experiences its own nāda. Nāda is classified in three parts viz. (1) parānāda (2) Mahānāda (3) the Nāda resulting from the union of Bindu and Bija.[56]

The Bindu breaks itself into three parts, viz. (1) Bindu, Bija and Nāda. The Śiva aspect is predominant in Bindu, while in Nāda the elements of Śiva and Śakti both rules equally. The creative principles are evolved out of this supreme Bindu. In the creation Bindu serves the purpose of material cause; it is under the subject of Śakti according to the view of Śaiva-sect:[57].

The Taraka Up. asserts at the end that one who knows om would attain Avimuktam. It also mentions the om sound itself as the substitute of Rāma-mantra viz. "Om Rām Rāmāya namaḥ, Candrāya namo bhadrāya namaḥ" The Rāma worship exceeds to such a high extent that it is ranked to the grade of Om-worship. Om syllable is considered the most sacred one. It is the Brahman itself. The RU identifies here the Rāma with Om, the 'a' sound corresponding to Viśva, on the base of MNU[58] is equal to Lakṣmaṇa. The letter U of om (Taijasa) is compared to Śatrughna. The 'm' sound om, corresponds with Bharata, (Prājña) the half morce of Om is Rama and the entire Praṇava is identified with Sītā as mūla prakrti. This is a reference to the identification of individual soul with supreme soul, personified as Rāma.

Deussen opines that Ramottara-tāpini Up. is a later one but it imitates the Nṛsimha-Tapini. It is a revised model of the Nṛsimhatāpini; but it preaches the Rama cult.[59] It is not a uniform and consistant but from two or three Ups. the ideas are gathered and are formed under the name of Up. The text of Rāmottara tāpini is also similar to the Tāraka and Jābāla Up.[60]

The Jābāla[61] shows that Ātman is found in Avimukta. Avimukta place is to be searched between the varaṇā and Nāsi. The meaning of both the words are explained in it.

Varṇā is one which casts off all the faults committed by the body-organs while Nasi is so called because it destroys all the sins comitted by the body-organs. The meeting place between the eye-brows and nose is the Avimukta place, so far this is also the meeting place between the heavenly world and the highest world. (of the Ātman).

Yājñavalkya explains the Tāraka mantra to Bharadvāja.[62] The Tāraka mantra is constituted of six syllables with रेफ and बिन्दु. ॐ and रां are identified with each other. They have importance of same value. Referring to Rāma-Tattva, रां is a Praṇava and puruṣottama-rāma is a para-brahma. It has four parts. Lakṣmaṇa, Śatrughna, Bharata and Śri-Rāma. The four togetherly comprise Rama-tattva. Though paramatman is one, four parts are imagined to give a full idea about (1) Jāgrat (2) Svapna (3) Suṣupti (4) Viśuddha Brahma Lakṣmaṇa is identified with a of the Praṇava. He presides over jāgrat (gross world), he is like saṁkarṣaṇa. Śatrughna presides over Svapna and Taijasarupa. He is identical with 'u' in Praṇava. Then Bharata is identified with 'm', presides over prajnā-rūpa. Śri-Rāma is a ardhamātrā and he is Puruṣottama. On account of the association with Śri-Rāma, that power which rules over utpatti, pālan and saṁhāra, is identical with the Sītā is of nādabindu svarupa.

GU.

The conversation between Durvāsas and Rādhā makes Durvāsas narrate the story of the incarnation of Gopāla Kṛṣṇa. It is as follows-once upon a time Nārāyaṇa was pleased with Brahmā's devotion and gave him a boon viz. asking of free question to Nārāyaṇa. In the story narrated in the GU. the reason of being pleased is not told as in the case of the stories in the BHP.

The GU describes Mathurā-nagarī in relation with the best incarnation among all the incarnations, Lord Nārāyaṇa, the granter of the boon, told that there are seven sacred places on this earth, viz., Ayodhyā, Mathurā, Māyā, Kāñchi, Kāśi, Avantikā and Dvāraka, Parallel to those of seven sacred cities of Indra and other gods. Among these cities Mathurā, the city of Gopāla Kṛṣṇa, is the best one. In it Gopāla Kṛṣṇa resides[63] and all the desires of the obtainer are fulfilled according to the degree of the spiritual develoment.

Mathurā is compared with a lotus, standing in a lotus-pond. It is the actual Brahman. It is protected by Viṣṇu's discus. Mathurā is surrounded by various vanas (forests)[64] like Big Bṛhad-vana, the Madhu-Vana, the Tal-vana, the Bahula. The Kumuda-vana, the Khādira-vana, the Bhadra-vana, the Bhāṇdirā-vana, the Śri-vana, the Loha-vana and the Bṛndā-vana. The Varāh Purāṇa [65] and Nāradiya Purāṇa[66] also mentions 12 forests near Mathurā viz. Madhu, Tāl, Kumuda, Kāmya, Bahula, Bhadra, Khādira, Mahāvana, Loha-jaṅgha, Bilva, Bhāndira, Vṛndāvana. The Tīrthaṅka describes most of 12 forests expcept Śri-vana as compared to those of GU.[67] It is as follows : (1) Madhuvana—It has temples of catur-bhuja, Kumar-kalyāna, and Dhruva; and a cave of Lavaṇasura; and also a seat of Vallabhācarya, it has कृष्ण कुण्ड. It is 4,5 miles from Mathurā. Mahauli is the present name of Madhu-vana. Madhuvana is found round the Mahauli. It is 4 or 5 kilometres from modern Mathura. On the south-west side of it. The stream of Yamunā river was flowing near the modern Mathurā at the time of Ancient India.

(2) *Tāla-vana*—The temple of Baladeva is built up here; Balarāma killed Dhenukāsura. बाणभद्र कुण्ड is in it. It is called Tārasi-gāma.

(3) *Kumudavana*—It has a temple of Kapila-Muni, Seat of Vallabha, Śri-Vitthala, and Vihāra Kuṇḍa. One has to return to Mathurā again.

(4) *Bahulavana*—It is situated near the present 'Bāthi' village. It has temples of kṛṣṇa, Balarāma, Bahula cowherds and a seat of Vallabhācārya; a Kṛṣṇa Kuṇda.

(5) *Kāmavana*—A temple of goddess Vṛndā-Devi in the temple of Govind. It has 84 Kuṇḍas viz. Madhu-sudan Kuṇḍa. Yaśoda Kuṇḍa etc. The five Pāṇḍavas spent their vanavāsakāla at this place (Kamavana).

(6) *Vṛndāvana*—The story is told how this place is called Vṛndāvana. Vṛndā, the daughter of Mahārāja Kedar performed penance for getting Kṛṣṇa as her husband. Kṛṣṇa pleased with her and appeared before her. Vṛndāvana is a holy place. Secondly Rādhā-Kṛṣṇa played Lilā here and the presiding deity is Vṛndādevi. So it is named Vṛndāvana. It is miles from Mathurā towards the north of Mathurā. The Vṛndāvana was a very vast region from Govardhana, Nandagāma, Barsana upto Kamavana at the time of the Lord Kṛṣṇa.

(7) *Bhadra-vana*—It has a temple of Madhusudana and icon of Hanumāna, and also a Madhusudana Kuṇḍa.

(8) *Bhāṇdir-vana*—It has Bhāṇdiravata, Bhāṇdira-well and crown. The story is told that (i) Rādhākṛṣṇa were married in this place by Brahmā according to purāṇas.

(9) *Bela-vana*—It has the temple of Lakmi and a seat of Vallabhācārya.

(10) *Loha-vana*—It has a temple of Gopināthaji and a cave of Lohāsura and a Kṛṣṇa Kuṇḍa. It is told that in it Kṛṣṇa killed Lohāsura.

(11) *Bṛhad-vana*—It is a wide forest but now the old.

Around Mathurā four temples of Śiva are found viz.

the Bhūteśvara on the west; the Pippaleśvara on the east, the Raṅgeśvara on the south and Gokarṇeśvara on the North.[68]

The GU describes that in these 12 forests, the celestials Gandharvas, Nagas, Kinnaras and men sang the praise of Kṛṣṇa all over the time. In these places the twelve Ādityas, the eleven Rudras, the eight Vasus, the seven sages, the five Vināyakas, the eight Lingas reside. Thus these places are most sacred. In such holy places the Siddhas also secure salvation. Among these forests, the Kṛṣṇa-vana and the Bhadra-vana are supposed to be the main forests. the icons of Kṛṣṇa, Balarāma, pradymna are found in Mathurā city. The Lord Kṛṣṇa is indicated by the four names. He is the 'Om-kāra'. The seeker gets the state of Brahma, if he meditates as "I am Gopāla, the paramātmana.[69] The worshipper of Kṛṣṇa overcome death. They become free from birth, death; they are released. He recognises the Go-pa-s.

The GU describes the bodily form of Kṛṣṇa beautifully. Kṛṣṇa has a distinguishing mark of the Śri-vatsa. His feet are marked with the desings of the divine banner; he has four hands with conch, the disc, the Śārṅga-bow, the lotus flower and the mace; the Keyuras shine on the upper arms, the crown on his head and the garlands on his neek. He shines with the lusture of gems, the makara earing adorn his ears, having the golden complexion with the right hand Kṛṣṇa assumes the abhaya pose, holding the flute in his hands. One should meditate on this type of image i.e. Kṛṣṇa in the form of Viṣṇu. The meditation on Him leads to the state of Kaivalya.

Śri-vatsa manifests the form of radiance of Brahman; The sun, fire, speech and the Moon, that radiance is called the Kaustubha-gem. The four arms of Viṣṇu constitute rhythm, mobility, inertia and individuality, Sattva, Rajas, Tamas, and Ahankar are four hands. The wise knows that the conch having the charactor of five elements, partakes the property of mobility, is in one hand (of Viṣṇu); the disc is purity of mind, the Śārṅga corresponds to the original Māyā, the lotus corresponds to the name of Viśva; it is placed in another hand. The upper arms are decorated with beautiful bracelets which constitute upright conduct Opulence and right desire (leading) to salvation. The garland is compared with Māyā, the pair of ear-rings is considered to be made of pearls which are produced from the radiant milk of the ocean of milk.

The lord Kṛṣṇa is indicated by the four names viz.

(1) Balrāma, is the Viśvātman, arises out of the letter 'A' of the Praṇava.

(2) Pradyumna is considered as Taijas, arising out of the letter 'U' of the Praṇava.

(3) Aniruddha is the prajñātman corresponding to the letter 'M' of Praṇava and

(4) Kṛṣna is a Turihya corresponding to ardhamatra (Bindu) of the Praṇava on whom the entire universe depends. Rukmini is the Śakti of Kṛṣṇa, the Mūlaprakṛti. This is how Go-pāla arising out of Om-Kāra is firmly established in the universe.

KLU

The sage Aśvalāyna requested the Brahmā to teach him the Brahmavidyā which is excellent mystic to the lord Brahmā. This Up. points out the sādhanā catuṣṭaya for salvation. It is not stated that Aśvalāyana possessed these four means of emancapation and the Sādhanā catuṣṭaya makes entitled for the achievement of the Brahmavidyā. The UP. is not clear about what is meant by Sādhanā catuṣṭyaya.

The lord Brahmā advised to attain freedom through Śraddhā (faith), Bhakti (devotion), Dhyāna (meditation) and Yoga. It is through sannyasa alone that renunciation is obtained and not by Karma, wealth, Vedāntavijñāna, tapas, purification of mind help for the realisation of paramātman. A sannyāsin who has completely given up desires for material objects, and given up the duties in the life, enters the Svarga; in the cave of the heart, (Dahara). He attains the highest self.

The Up, points out the body-posture of all ascetic. The ascetic sits in a pleasant posture, with his neck, head and body erect and subjugates all the passions.[70] He devotes and contemplates on heart (lotus) as being free from Rajo-guṇa.

He attains the paramesvara who is pure, sorrowless, invisible, unthinkable, endless, formless and source of Māyā. The paramātman is the innermost, self of all beings. He is not a subject of utpatti, sthiti and laya, He is unborn, indestructible, and omnipresent. He is present in gross as well as in subtle forms. He is called Viṣṇu Parāṇa, time, fire, Moon etc. He is all that exists and that will exist. The thing does not exist, if there is no presence of God.[71] Having known Him the person crosses death. A ritualistic example is given to show how a person's ignorance disappears viz. "Having constituted his body on Arani (the lower attritioned piece of wood) and Praṇava, the upper Arani, a wise man burns Ajñāna by the churning of meditation." The Brahman is beyond thinking or imagining limits of a man. To realise His nature fully is difficult. He is that Sadāśiva who is other than enjoyer, enjoyed and enjoyment. All emanate from Him, All exists in Him, All are absorbed in Him.[72] He is the atom of atoms. He is Jyotiṣām Jyotiḥ.[73] The Lord possesses some kind of power which is called Māyā in the KLU. And the Paramātman assumes a body with internal organs and behaves accordingly due to Māyā. In the dreaming state the jiva enjoys pleasures and pains which are created by his Māyā.

One who realises such Brahman attains the pure form of Paramātman. The KLU also speaks the Brahman in the form of Sadāśiva having the body viz. the dark blue throat.

the recitaton of this Up. makes the person like Agni, i.e. to say he becomes lustrous like fire. He is free from the duties of the four orders of life. The sins like theft of gold, drinking etc. become futile, he acquires the wisdom that destroys the ocean of Saṁsāra. Having known Him the person obtains Kaivalya-state.

The Up. preaches that the knowledge of the Highest self is nothing but knowledge of one's self. A person experiences "He is that one", such kind of knowledge relieves him from all bondage. The Up. also stresses the point that the knowledge of Brahman is impossible without devotion. the path of devotion is praise worthy in many ways. It is free from all obstacles. Everybody is entitled to follow it. Detachment towards the worldly enjoyment is the condition for spiritual development.

Maitreya Up. of the Sv.

The beginning portion of this story resembles with the opening portion of the MAU; but the Maitreya of the Sv. differs from the Maitrāyaṇi Up. of the Yv.[74] It deals with the two characters, viz. the king Bṛhadraṭha, and the sage Śākāyanya. The king is represented as being aloof from the worldly objects. According to him the body is impermanent and so he wishes to renounce everything. He leaves the kingdom in the hands of his son, and goes to the ferest. There he performed severe tapas. At the end Śākāyanya, who looked like fire without smoke, came in front of him. The sage said to the king, "Rise, Rise and choose a boon." The king requested him to enlighten him on the sattva (i.e. the state of Sat or Brahman.). The sage tried to divert him on some other desire. It may be noted that like all other Ups. This Upaniṣatkāra considers that the problems regarding the knowledge of Brahman are difficult to answer.

The king prostrates before the sage and begs to make

him free from the cycle of rebirth. The king is quite confident that the sage will make him free from the bondage of saṁsāra.

The sage blessed him that he would be Atmajñāni. He would be famous by the name of Marut. He describes the Atman as follows:— sound, touch and other seem to be artha, but in fact they are anartha (evil). They result into anartha. The Bhutātman (lower self) clings to these organs always. He never resembles to the Supreme one. The sattva (quality) is possible to have through the tapas. The sattva makes the mind pure and by means of the pure mind the Ātman can be attained, when one attains Ātman, he gets liberation. It is the citta (thought) alone that is Saṁsāra. It is affected by the sense-objects by the events that occur. It should be cleansed with efforts. It should be purified and this leads to the destruction of the karmas.

The Parameśvara is light, eternal unchangable, undual. He cannot be grasped by the mind. He is the only witness for the playings of buddhi. He is not connected with anything. He looks upon this universe as a jugglery.

The ignorant observes the orders of the caste system which result into the beginning and the end. the Up. stresses on the point that one should dwell in that endless and most supreme Bliss having given up the identification with sons as well as the body.

PU. (Praṇavopniṣad)

The PU. narrates a story about the significance of the mystic sound 'Om'. Once the Asuras besieged the city of Indra. At that time the gods were afraid and began to think as to who would kill the Asuras when they saw the oṁkāra, the elder son of Brahma, the gods requested him to be their leader to conquer the Asuras. then by putting a condition to them omkara received a boon that Om would be uttered at the beginning. A Brahmin could not utter the Vedas without taking his name first; otherwise chanting the veda by a Brahmin would be invain. Afterwards the gods defeated the Asuras.

The PU. refers to the grammatical part of the Om. Indra asked Prajāpati when he (Indra) praised him (Prajāpati). All the questions of the Indra are related to the grammatical part. viz. (1) which metre is of Om. (2) Its gender (3) its svara, (4) its preposition; (5) its case, (6) its colour; (7) its definition; (8) its letters; (9) words therein; (10) its place and (11) way of being propounded.

The Up. propounds that the Om is one single syllable. It is uttered in various ways according to different vedas. In the Rv. the Om consist of three vowels is already Uddāta; In the Yv, Om which is a single syllable consists of dirgha uddāta and a pluta uddāta in the Sv. Om, which consists of three vowels is a hrsva uddata; in the Av. which has two padas, consists 'उ' (U) as anudatta and अ (A) as Uddata. It is said in the PU. that the first mora of the Om is of the red colour; the second mora 'u' is of the black colour; and the third mora 'm' is of brown colour and the fourth mora which is half is of white colour. The Up. also narrates the rewards of meditation on each mora. i.e. to say (1) One who meditates on the first mora secures Brahma's state, the meditation on the second mātrā leads to the Viṣṇu's state (3) the third one produces the effect of the Īśana state. And that which fourth one leads to the Brahman's state. It includes all the deities.

Then follows the AUM's definition. The word is made from the root āp. to pervade thus Om means "which pervades all. According to some it is derived from the root ava. In nipātas Om is called "Ukṣatta" by the grammarians. It is a kṛdanta in prātipadikas. It is an avyaya. It has all the three genders, all the cases; all the case-terminations do not apply to the Om syllable. It is undeclinable. The Om is formed by replacing the second syllable first and the first in the place of second viz. a u m u a m (Om = ओम्). 'o' is velar 'm' is uttered with the help of two lips. The fourth mora is an intermediate letter which has to two lips as its articulators. The first letter has open (विवृत) effort; the second letter is stop.

The Gāyatri is the metre of Om; it has four Vyāhṛtis viz.

The author of the Up. brings out the significance of the utterance of Om; if Om is meditated one gets the lusture back if he loses it due to some or other mistake in a chanting or in a ritual, thus Om is worshipped at the beginning of a mantra.

The author of the Up. devotes one full Up. to the single syllable "Om". It seems that the Praṇava worship must have reached its highest peak at that time. No doubt the Om is praised in various Ups. It is considered the Supreme Self itself. The worship of 'Om' is entitled to give the reward of Brahman's realisation. It produces the effect of blissful state, which is devoid of fear or worldly agitations.The MNU[75] discusses the sound Om widely. The GK[76] also identifies the mystic sound Om with all that, Om is all this, what was what is and what will be. It is considered Brahman, Itself. It is the unmanifest cause of the manifest universe. The GK[77] calls it the Lord who is ever present in the minds of all. It includes all the sounds of all the symbols, Om is always praised as the most significant and fruitful one. It is the substratum of birth, growth and decay.[78] The MU[79] compares the 'Om' or 'Praṇava' with the bow. A nice metaphor is woven around the sacred syallable Om. viz. The Om syllable is a bow; the individual soul is an arrow; the target of its shot is Brahman. The target is to be unerringly hit. Then the goal is achieved. One secures the union with Brahman. the KATU[80] states that all the vedas declare, all the penances proclaim the one single goal and that is the 'Om'. The Praśna Up.[81] also sets forth the Om as a means of highest meditation, by which a wise man secures the highest Brahman. Ś gives much importance to this sacred syllable. and ranks Om as a nearest stay of Brahman.[82] this mystic syllable is recognised in the Ups.

The MNU expounds the significance of "Om" and identifies Om with the aspects of the Self, and proceeds to the realisation of Brahman. The Up. does not refer to the grammatical discussion on the Om but it propounds the non-duality through the worship of Om. this Up. declares:—There are three forms (quarters) (1) waking, (ii) dream. (iii) sleep respectively in which the self appears. The fourth mora is Turiya, the absolute Brahman. The GK. also compares Om on the line of MNU; it is but natural when MNU constitutes the basic text for the GK. It proceeds to explain the three states of experience. The Śruti identifies the waking state with 'A' letter of Om. Both of them are compared because both have a common point for comparison viz. "All pervasiveness or being the first. The sound "A" is the very foremost sound. All sounds are pervaded by "A". Lord Kṛṣṇa also puts forth the importance of "A" in all the letters by saying: "He is "A" in the letters."[83] The Vaisvanara pervades the entire universe. The first state is called "Viśva". The GK. adds the seat for Viśva to MNU's śruti. The Gk. locates the Viśva in the right eye.

"u" the second letter of this monosyllable is compared with the Taijasa because it is a mid-way between the Viśva and the Prājña. the place for Taijasa or dreamself is manas. they are compared because "Superiority"; or intermediate state is a common feature in both of them. The letter "U" comes after the letter "A", therefore there is superiority; similarly the Taijasa or the dreamer is Superior to Viśva because the experiences in waking state are antecdent to the dream. The third letter viz. "M" is compared with the Prājña or the deep-sleep, since in both the "measure" and "becoming one" are the common qualities. All other sounds are absorbed in "M" while chanting AUM. Moreover A and U rises up again from M. similarly the experience of the dream state and the waking state ceases into the deep sleep and the sleep superceeds. In both the carlier plurality and variedness merge to become one as a whole. The Prājña is located in the either of the heart. These three viz. Viśva, Taijasa and Prājña are one fundamentally. And all of them are present in the waking state also. The self is observed as threefold in one body.

The person who is able to understand or to judge the happening both within and without him, becomes able to comprehend the knowledge, however hard and complicated may be. A meditator of Om is benefitted with the rewards as mentioned in the GK.[84] The soundless part of Om does not produce any reward in this finite world. In chanting Om, the blissful moment or silence arises between the second and the first chanting. This is the fourth mora of Om which is the same as Ātman. The soundless part of the Om is the goal of the meditator. In crresponds to the pure Ātman. In silence the sense organs do not notice impression. The mind does not comprehend the assumptions. It is engrossed in the worship. This is the experience of the Turīya. The fourth state when the mind is made single pointed by chanting. The other thoughts do not appear. The mind becomes unified, absorbed in Om vibrations. Thus om being Brahman, one experiences Brahman, the all pervading truth, the eternal One. The experience of oneness is blissful. The effort in the spiritual Sādhanā is to stop the production of the thoughts, to regulate the flow of thinking, One is benefitted by making the mind steady in Om-worship, from all the limitations, agitations and finite world.

REFERENCES

1. BG. 13.15.
2. Iśa. Up. 5.
   "Tadantarasya sarvasya tadu sarvasyāsyabāhyataḥ."
3. Iśa. 2.
4. KATU 1.10
5. vide Radhakrishnan, S., The Principal Upanishads, CHU, p. 428.
6. Vide Appendix No.1.
7. Cf. BG. 5.10 Lipyate na sa pāpena padmapatramivāmbhasā.
8. BRU 6.2.4 "Varam bhagavate Gautamāya dadhma iti."
9. CHU 5.3.6
10. CHU 5.3.6
11. Vide Kane, P.V., History of Dharmashastra Vol.V PII, p.1548-1560
12. ibid
13. Cf. Deussen, Sixty Upanishads of the Veda, (translated by) Bedekar and Palsule G.B. Vol. I, p.138.
14. Vide, Max Muller, Bṛhādaraṇyaka Upanishad (6.2.7), p. 206. SBE Vol. 25, p.206.
15. BRU. 4.3.6.
16. (i) TB. 3.12.9.7
    (ii) BG. 15.12.
    (iii) CHU 3.13.7
17. Modern scientist like george Meek adopts the Yājñavalkya's technique, viz. "From visible to invisible", vide Life Beyond, Vol VIII, No. 5, p. 5.11
18. Cf. George Meek classifies the mind in three levels:
    (1) Superconscious (2) Conscious (3) Subconscious
19. Op. cit. Life Beyond Vol. VIII. George Meak agrees with the Upaniṣadic Viewpoint viz. The soul takes new form and begins new life, after its death.
20. BRU. 1.3.28. 'tamaso ma jyotir gamaya'.
21. Vide, Belvalkar S.K. and Ranade R.D. Creative period, p. 183.
22. Radhakrishnan, S., The Principle Upanishads., p. 163 on "Abhyāroha"
23. Belvalkar, S.K. and Ranade, R.D., "Creative period", p.183.
25. The modern scientist George Meek also takes the question about "Life after death" is highly subtle. Moreover he agrees with the Upaniṣadic view viz. It is beyond the scope of mental understanding, intellectual capacity, comprehension emotional feeling and practical experience of an average man.
    cf Meek's article in 'Life Beyond' Vol. III. N.5, p.5.

26. Vide Swami Ranganathananda, "The message of the Upanishads, p.292.
27. Op. cif, Swami Ranganathananda, "The message of the Upanishads, P. 293.
28. cf. IŚU 7.
29. KATU. 2.17.
30. CHU. 7.23.
31. MU. 3.1.
32. KATU 2.3.14.
33. Gārgyāyaṇi is read as Gaṅgyāyaṇi. Deussen and S. Radhakrishnan accepts the reading Gaṅgyāyaṇi. Many editions including Ānandāśrama (1859) follow the reading Gārgyāyaṇi. All the Telegu MS, read Gārgyāyaṇi throughout.
34. Vide Radhakrishnan, S., The Principal Upanishads, p. 789.
35. Taking Samit in hands is a sign of showing social custom, humbleness, desirous of learning.
36. When a person approaches to other person in order to draw the attention towards himself utters peculiar words. Compare Manusmrti II. 124 ft, it mentions some custom viz. how a Brahmin salutes to the other person telling his name.
37. vide Meek George, "Life Beyond Vol. III N.5., p. 5, ft. He also mentions the six planes corresponding to the six worlds mentioned in the KAU 1.1. The existence of six planes according to Meek is as follows: –
    1. Physical or earth plane
    2. Lowest Astral plane.
    3. Middle (Intermediate) Astral plane.
    4. Highest Astral plane.
    5. Mental and causal plane.
    6. Celestial plane.

    the scientist opines that every spirit has life in these planes. They are engaged in many works suitable to their development.
38. CHU 8.5.3, mentions "arah" which is full of aira. aira means enemies such as love-anger. The term āra denotes enemies i.e. love, happiness. The moments are called Yeṣṭiha. According to Maxmuller it means killing the sacrifices; which consists in a desire for Brahman. Cf. Deussen, He differs in translation e.g. ara: lake translates as the tossing flood. And yeṣṭihah means duration of sacrifice. vide Deussen, sixty Ups. Of Veda, translated by Bedekar V.M. and palsule G.B. Vol. I, p.27.

39. Deussen differs in translation. Ilya=rich with refreshing juice. vide Deussen; "Philosophy of sixty upanishads Vol. I p.27. According to Max Muller Ilya means the same tree as the Aśvattha.
40. Deussen differs in translation. Sālajya=protected with bow-strings as thick as the sāl trees. Belvalkar abopts the variant sallaja and renders it as the source of existence, sat: mergence-la, and emergence-ga. (Vide Belvalkar S.K., creative period p.27.)
41. Vicakṣaṇā—Visible from a far. Op. Cit. Deussen Paul, "Philosophy of Sixty Upanishads", translated by Bededkar, V.M., and palsule G.D. Vol.I.p.27.
42. Vide Radhakrishnan, S., "The principal Upanishads", p.789.
43. MU 1.2.5-6.
44. CHU 5.3.6 and BRU 6.2.5 ft.
45. Cf. BG. 8.23-27.
46. BG. 8.21.
47. Vide Deussen, Sixty Upanishads in veda vol.I (translated by Bedekar V.M. and palsule G.B.) KAU, p.46.
48. Belvalkar, S.K. and Ranade, R.D., Creative period p. 277.
49. Vide, Belvalkar S.K. and Ranade, R.D., Creative period, p. 313.
50. Cf. BRU 5.9; CHU 3.13.8.
51. Vide, Belvalkar S.K. and Ranade R. D., "Creative Period", p. 313.
52. Vide MNU—8 ft. And GK. 1.25 ft.
53. CHU 1.5.1; Rv. 10.190.3-4, KATU 6.1; 2.16.
54. vide Ranade, R.D., "Constructive Philosophy of the Upanishad, p. 39..
55. Vide M.M. Gopinath Kavirāj, " Paper on Nāda bindu and Kalā; J.G.J.R.I Voi.III part 2, p. 97 ft.
56. ibid.
57. ibid.
58. MNU K.8 ft.
59. Deussen, "Sixty Upanishads of Veda "Vol. II. (Translated by Bedekar V.M. and palsule G.B.) p. 879/
60. ibid., p. 879-880.
61 Jābāl-Up.2–सोडविमुक्तः कस्मिन् प्रतिष्ठित इति। वरणायां नास्यां च मध्ये प्रतिष्टिम इति का वे वरणा का च नासीति। सर्वानिन्द्रियकृतान् दोषान् वारयसीति तेन वरणा भवति। सर्वान्द्रियकृतान् पापान् नाशयतीति तेन नासी भवतीति। कतमच्चास्य स्थानं भवतीति। भुवोर्धाणस्य च यः संधि सरुष धोर्खेकस्य परस्य च संधिर्भवतीति। एतब्दै संधि संध्यां ब्रह्मविद उपासन इति सोडविमुक्त उपास्य इति। सोडविमुक्तं ज्ञानमाचष्टे यो वै तदेवं वेदेति।।2।।

62. Vide Kalyāna-Upanishad-aṇka, "Ramottara-tapini is explained and discussed fully."
63. Tirthāṅka: "Dhruva, son of Svayambhuva-Manu advised to meditate in Madhuvana and told-" पुण्यं मधुवनं यत्र सांनिध्यं नित्यदा हरे: "Madhuvana was the ancient name of Mathurā from ancient times it is a holy place. Kalyana Vol.31, p.95,1957.
64. Vide Kane P.V. " History of Dharmasastra" Vol. IV, p.690" the territory round Mathurā is extended 20 yojanas and the Mathurā city was in its midst."
65. Chap. 153 and 161 6-10.
66. Chap. Uttarardha 79-10-18.
67. Tirthaṅka mentions two forests more than to those of GU. viz. Gahvara-Vana and Vihara-vana. Thus the variation in the places may be observed. The difference in names of place may be due to the ancient names of those tracts rounds Mathurā.
    vide fn.1.
68. 'Tirthāṅka' Kalyāṇa vol.31 P.96H.
69. GU—15 "Sohamityatmanamadaya manasaikyam kuryāt"
70. cf. Svetasvetara Up.2.8.
    त्रिरून्नत स्थाप्य समं शरीरं तदीन्द्रियाणि मनसा संनिरूध्य।
    ब्रह्मेउपेन प्रक्षरेत विन्दान्स्त्रोक्षांसि सर्वाणि भयावहानि।।
71. Compare BG.10.39.
72. cf. Tu 3.1. "yato vā imāni bhutāni jāyante, Yena Jātāni jivanti."
73. BRU 4.3.6
74. Radhakrishnan, S., takes the Maitri and Maitrāyaṇi Up. belonging to Maitrayaniya branch of the black Yv. He remarks, "in some text it is assigned to the SV. vide Radhakrishnan, S., The principle Upanishad, p. 795. Belvalkar, S.K., disagrees with Radhakrishnan's view. He takes Maitri and Maitrāyaṇi Ups. as the two separate Ups. One belonging to Yv. while the other Maitri belongs to Sv. vide Belvalkar, S.K. and Ranade, R.D., "Creative period", p. 123. He remarks, "The Upanishad had to be carefully distinguished from two other similar Upanishadic texts—The Mai treya and Maitreyi.
75. MNU 8 ft.
76. GK1.25 ft.
77. (i) I.28, (ii) I.26 (iii) I.25 (i) Praṇavam hisvaram vidyat sarvasya hṛdi samsitam, sarvavyapinamoñkāra.
    (ii) Praṇava hiparam brahma, Praṇavaśca Paraḥ Smṛtaḥ.
    (iii) Praṇavo brahma nirbhayam

78. GK. I 27. Savrasya Pranavo hyadirmadyamantastathaiva ca.
79. MU. 2.2.4
80. KATU.1.2.15.
81. Praśna Up.V.7
82. cf. ŚBH on Praśna Up. v 7 "Nediṣṭhām hi ālambana oṁkāro-brahmaṇaḥ."
83. Vide BG. 10.33.
84. GK. I.23. "Akaro nayate viśvamukāraścāpi Taijasam... makāraśca punaḥ prājñam nāmātre vidyate gatiḥ"

CHAPTER V

COMMENTATORS

Introduction

The Ups. mainly deal with the inner 'Being' or with what is called the spiritual knowledge. The knowledge of the 'Self' can be distinguished from the knowledge of the material world. The Ups. are an earnest inquiry into the ultimate truth. The subject matter is about the spiritual life that leads to eternal peace and immortality. The Ups. revolt against the path of ritualism. The seers of the Ups. placed aside the performance of the sacrifices. while they emphasise the intellctual efforts to know the ultimate truth. As they propound philosophical thoughts, they serve as the source of different traditional philosophical thoughts.

The Ups. expound principles which can not be easily grasped or which cannot be experienced by everyone through the senses. On the contrary that highest priniciple is realisable only by those persons who become introvert through penance, meditation etc. and after their spiritual progress the truth reveals Itself to the person concerned.

This principle is exposed and explained vividly in various Ups. in various ways by the seers as they have realised It. All the Ups. expound the same principle but the way in which they establish the Brahman is different; so the number of commentaries are written on this subject to suit it. The BRS deals and discusses Upaniṣadic Śrutis. There are many commentaries on the BRS. The commentators systematically explain the varying docrtines of the Ups.

The commentator aims to give the consistent interpretation of the BRS according to his Philosophical ideology. The five principal Bhāṣyakāras viz. (1) Ś (2) R, (3) M (4) V (5) N; have developed their views on the basis of Ups. and interpret the BRS in relation to their philosophical ideas and views. They modify the Śrutis to suit their views. These great ācāryas founded their own schools. they try to explain the Śruti and try to co-relate the BRS according to their philosophical line of thinking.

The commentators discuss the Śrutis which suit to their philosophical thoughts, with the rational arguements. Such discussions are grasped by the intellectuals. The theories put forth by the commentators appealed to the highly educated people and thus their scholarship is recognised by these intellectuals. Similarly the commentators create the different ways of attracting the people from the religious point of view. Any ācārya preached his own thought in such a way which can be easily diagestible by all; which can be understood by a common man. The ācārya made the philosophy in a dialute form which suits to his line of thinking; and this simple approach, the way of the interpretation in easiest manner, captured the mind of a common person. The ācārya emphasised on the god by various symbols viz. Om etc. by the different stotras; by the ways of worship to the gods etc. which can be easily followed. Naturally a person knew how to achieve the god's grace and he came to know what Brahman means etc. Thus an ācārya collected the followers to his school.

The study of the Ups. show how a commentator has an ample scope to interpret the Upaniṣadic text in relation to the philosophical ideology which he represents. Thus it is worthwhile to examine how these five bhāṣyakāras expain their own view with the help of the Śrutis. From this point of view in the fifth chapter some of the Śrutis are taken up and explained according to Śaṅkara, Rāmānuja, Vallabha, Mādhva and Nimbārka. The words from the Śruti on the relevant portion are explained according to these bhāṣyakāras. The first section (A) of the fifth chapter deals with the explanation of the Śrutis by the above mentioned commentators. The complicated references and varied discussions on the relevant portion are not taken up while explaining the Śrutis.

In the section B of this Chapter the BRS is studied in relation to the explanations given by the five ācāryas. From the Śrutis which are under consideration the ācāryas draw their conclusions in the respective adhikaraṇa. Sometimes a parricular adhikaraṇa in the BRS discusses the Śrutis from different Ups. On the same subject. In this discussion it is show how the ācāryas reconcil various Śrutis. The Section contains what is relevant of the present discussion. The main teaching of the ancient ācāryas, as presented in the adhikaraṇas are set not fort. Thus the section serves as a background to the stories and dialogues as well as the teachings of the Ups. The commentators and the BRS are studied in this section in order to see how far they contribute to the concept of the vara (boon) which is dealt in the Chapter I. The attempt is done in order to examine whether these great ācāryas add more or not to the concept or they merely go on discussing and drawing the conclusions.

The original bhāṣyas of these five ācāryas on all the Ups. are not available. The Rāmānuja's bhāṣya on the CHU, BRU, KATU is not available; so the portion on the above mentioned Ups. is studied with the help of the Raṅgarāmānujabhāṣya. The Raṅgarāmānuja has written the commentary on the basis of Rāmānuja's views; so it is taken into account. Śaṅkara and Madhva's Bhaṣya on CHU, BRS and KATU is available.

The portion on these above mentioned Ups. are studied

with the help of the Śaṅkara and Madhva. Vallabha's bhāṣya on any one of the relevant Ups. in not found. K A U is studied with the help of Śaṅkarānanda's bhāṣya on the MAU, Rāmatirtha's bhāṣya is available so it is studied with ther help of Rāmatirtha's commentary.

The chart showing the functional similarities on the basis of the bhāṣyas of the five great ācāryas, viz., Śaṅkara, Rāṁanuja. Vallabha, Madhva, is added in this thesis. Deussen has given a chart showing the pañcāgnividyā from the ŚB-14.9.1-12-16 to the CHU 5.3.9; and the BRU 6.2.9-13.[1]

The CHU and the BRS are dealt by N.A. Kansara[2] and he tries to conclude that almost all the five ācāryas agree with the explanation of the process by which the water is called 'Puruṣa' after the fifth oblation.

CHU 5.3.6...I Agni Dyulokaḥ

Fire	*Fuel : Sun*	*Smoke : Rays*	*Flame : Day*	*Coals : Moon*	*Sparks : Stars*	*Oblation : Faith*	*Result*
Ś Asau lokaḥ	Ś brings out the similarity in the Sun and the fuel. The similarity consists in the brightness. In the sacrificial fire when the fuel is added like wood, ghee, oil, it illuminates the ritual more strongly, so also the Sun lights up the heaven more brightly.	Here is a similarity between the smoke and the rays, when the fire burns profusely the flames come out of it. In case of the heaven rays are flames because they are the effect of the Sun and have also the quality of brightness.	When the fire burns profusely the flames come out of it. In case of heaven days are flames because they are the effect of the Sun and have also the quality of brightness.	The moon is compared here with the coal, The moon becomes visible when the day is over; the coal becomes visible when the flame ceases.	The stars are the sparks because they are like the parts of the moon.	In this metaphor the faith is the oblation.	Soma
Rg	R follows Ś in the explanation.						
M Heaven is Vāsudeva	The similee is of the fire altar. The Sun is the lord; the highest manifestation. The Lord appears as the Sun. The Sun gives	The Vāsudeva is compared with the dhuma. It is the terrific form of the Lord. The rays that proceed from	The Saṁkarṣaṇa form of the Lord is called the day; He is arcis. Arcis also means the	The moon in the heaven is Pradyumna form of the Lord. The aṅgāra means the	The Aniruddha is the form of the Lord, since He is the inspirer. The sparks also means the		

Fire	*Fuel : Sun*	*Smoke : Rays*	*Flame : Day*	*Coals : Moon*	*Sparks : Stars*	*Oblation : Faith*	*Result*
	light to the world. So also the lord gives light to the world. It is the Nārāyaṇa-samit also means the highest manifestation.	the Sun; by the vibration of these rays all evil is destroyed.	adorable.	thriller.	inspirer.		
	Thus the Lord appears in his five forms in the heaven.						

II—"Parjanya"

Fire	*Fuel : Wind*	*Smoke : Cloud*	*Flame : Lightening*	*Coal : aśani*	*Sparks : Thunder of the clouds*	*Oblation : Soma*	*Result*
Ś parjanya as the Presiding deity of the rain	The Samit is wind because through the force of the wind the rain falls; when the fuel is added the fire burns profusely, so also in the case of 'Parjanya' happens; because of the force of the wind the rain falls.	The smoke and the clouds both resemble in black colour.	The lightening and flame possess brightness. That is why they are compared.	The coal and the aśani both have hardness and also have contact with lightening.	The thunder of the clouds is called ह्रादनयः because both have the common quality of scattering.	In this metaphor Soma is the oblation.	Rain
Rg—	He agrees with the interpretation of Ś in taking rain as Presiding deity and 'ह्रादनयः' as the noise made by clouds.		R leaves on the reader to understand the functional similarities about other constituents. He does not explain each and every word. He says i.e. "शिष्टं स्पष्टम्"[1]				
M—	According to M's view in the Second oblation the Jīva gets another coating. The Soul has now two Sheaths (1) The mental (2) astral. The two atoms now become active. Further he tells that the soul is called Sraddha, instead of the water. The five stages in the Soul's rebirths meant here : the first stage is the entrance of the Soul i. Soma world. This is the first oblation.						

1. vide रङ्गरामानुज भाष्य on the CHU. 5.5.1-2 : viz.
अत्र वाय्यादीनां समिदादिकल्पना निमित्तं यथायोग्यमन्वेषणीयम्।
द्युलोकयोग.........मेघमण्डो॰ पततीत्यर्थः। (शिष्टं स्पष्टम्)।

III—Pṛthivi

Fire	*Fuel : Year*	*Smoke : Space*	*Flame : Night*	*Coals : Directions*	*Sparks : Intermediate directions*	*Oblation : Rain*	*Result : Food*
Pṛthivi Ś—	The earth shines through the year with its manifold seasons having produced the grains like wheat, rice etc. Just as the samit brightens and kindles the fire similarity the year makes the earth shining through the manifold seasons by producing the grains like wheat, rice etc.	The space and the smoke both have similarity in having the source for rising; the space seems to be risen from the earth; just as the rises from the smoke fire.	The earth and the night both depend on other factors to illuminate them The night is brightened through the moon. It never possesses the Self brightness. Moreover the night and the earth are considered as having tamas (darkness) quality.	The Diśa and the aṅgāra both have pacified nature as a common factor.	Both of them are least concerned, they do not have much importance.	In this metaphor the rain is the oblation.	food
Rg.—	In the third oblation the soul enters into the plants which are food for man.		According to R—	The flame is night because both reason-resemble in the colour viz. blue.			
M—	He keeps silence about mentioning the similarity between remaining Constituents. In the third oblation the soul enters into the plants i.e. which are food of man.						

IV—Puruṣa

Fire Puruṣa	*Fuel : Speech*	*Smoke : Vital breath*	*Flame : Tongue*	*Coal : Eyes*	*Sparks : Ears*	*Oblation : Food*	*Result : Retas*
Ś	Just as a samit kindles the fire and throws light around it, the speech of a man impresses on the other person. It throws light on his personality.	The Prāṇa and the smoke both of them have some character viz. production from a substratum. The Prāṇa comes out of its abode viz. (Mukha).	The tongue and the flame both resemble in sameness of the colour. The redness of a tongue is compared with flame.	The eyes and coals both possesses same quality of vision and so they are here compared	Both of them have common feature of scattering and so the ears are called the sparks	In this metaphor the 'food' is the oblation	Retas
Rg	He agrees with Ś' explanation for the first constituent but he does not mention other similarities. He remarks as follows :— एवमन्याः द्रष्टव्यम्।						
M	—						

V—Yoṣa (Woman)

Fire Yoṣa	*Fuel : Speech*	*Smoke : Vital breath*	*Flame : Tongue*	*Coal : Eyes*	*Sparks : Ears*	*Oblation : Food*	*Result : Retas*
Ś	Just as a samit shines through kindling, similarly a woman shines because of a birth of child	Upa mantra ṇa means the act of inviting. A woman is a wise of Upamantraṇa; just as the smoke is a cause of Agni.	They are compared because both are similar in colour.	What is done inside and the coal both posses the quality of a fire; and so antaḥkaraṇa is called the coal.	Just as the sparks are produced for a short time and they disappear within a moment. Similarly the delights of the sexual satisfation are momentary. They rise, exist and disappear within a short time.	In this metaphor the Retas is the oblation	
Rg	He takes उपमन्त्रणम् as संकेतकरणम्. He agrees with Ś'						

Br. Up. 6.2.9-13 I—Dyulokaḥ

Fire	*Fuel : Sun*	*Smoke : Rays*	*Flame: Day*	*Coal: Quarter*	*Sparks: Quarter intermediate quarters*	*Oblation*	*Result*
Ś *Ś*	Just as samit (fuel) kindles and enlightens the fire, the Sun enlightens that world. That is why the Sun is called as samit.	The smoke and rays both have the similarity of being risen from the fuel; it is known that the rays emanate from the Sun and similarly smoke comes out of fuel.(like oil, ghee, wood etc.)	The flame and day both are bright, both are compared being alike through manifestation.	Both represent a pacified state. Space, like cinder has heat or lusture. That is why the quarters are called the coals.	They are scattered like sparks just as the sparks scatter from the fire, so also the other quarters scatter and so they are called sparks.	The gods sacrifice in this fire. The word Devaḥ to mean the human organs of vision, etc. the Somaraja the form which performers and institutors of sacrifices assume after death.	Soma.
R	He Agrees with Ś interpretation.	The rays are produced from the 'आदित्य रूप समिन्'	Gives same explanation like Ś.	-	-		
M	Differs from Ś & Rg. M does not	The Viṣṇu is called dhuma	The Viṣṇu is called archi	The Viṣṇu is called	The Viṣṇu is called the		

Fire	*Fuel : Sun*	*Smoke : Rays*	*Flame : Day*	*Coa l: Quarter*	*Sparks : Quarter intermediate quarters*	*oblation*	*Result*
	take the five constituents in physical fire but all are connected with the five Manifestations of the Lord: 1. Viṣṇu is called samit because He is super excellent. (Sam-Super, it-edha-excellent).	because He causes all evil-doers to tremble. (dhu means to tremble. He derives the world dhuma from dhu to tremble.	because He is the most adored one. He interpretes the word arch as follow—arch -most and chata-adore.	angār be-cause he delights in the bo-dies of all jivas. Aṅga means body and Rati means delight according to M.	sparks because he flashes on the wise,in diverse ways.		
First Fire	He is called Āditya because he is essentially wisdom and life.	He is Abhra because He is the support of the waters.	He is Vidyut He enlightens all.	He is aśani because He eats up all.	He is always cheerful.		
Vallabh (V)	'āditya'—Sun	Kiraṇa (Rays)	Day (aha)	Moon	Nakṣatra.	Devas offer Soma as oblation.	It Pro-duces Soma king.

II—'Parjanya'

Fire	*Fuel : Year*	*Smoke : Cloud*	*Flame: Lightening*	*Coals : aśani*	*Sparks : Rumbling of the clouds*	*Obiation : The gods sacrifice in this fire* सोमोराजा	*Result. vṛṣti*
Ś	Just as fuel kindles and brightens the fire so also the rain god. Shines through all the six 'ṛtus' (Śarad, Griṣma, Hemant etc.) That is why the year is called the saint 'पर्जन्य' revolves with its parts.	Clouds are considered as Smoke from their similar (cloudy) appearance with Smoke. Both of them are blackish	Vidyut and 'arci' both are luminous. Both having the power of manifestation Both are compared.	Both represent a pacified state and are hard. Both being alike exitinguishable and hard. They are compared.	The rumblings of the clouds are sparks because both scattered and are numerous.		
Rg He seems 'पर्जन्य' as 'वृष्टि' प्रवर्तकोदवे:	The year having six 'ṛtus' illuminates The Parjanya.	He remains silent about the explanation of other constituents i.e. 'dhuma' 'arcis' 'aṅgāra'			He cites the meaning of 'विस्फुलिंग' as विप्रकीर्ण त्वानेकत्व सामान्यात् and ह्रादुनय: as स्तनार्यतुशब्दा:		

Fire	*Fuel : Year*	*Smoke : Cloud*	*Flame : Lightening*	*Coals : aśani*	*Sparks : Rumbling of the clouds*	*obiation The gods sacrifice in this fire* सोमोराजा	*Result. vṛṣti*
M	Do not differ from CHU's explanation.						
Vallabha	'Vāyu' - wind	'abhra'- Cloud	'vidyut'-lightening	'vajra' Thunder bolt	'nadi' River	In it Soma is offered as oblation.	'varṣa' is the fruit of it.
V	Differs from the Upaniṣadic Text.						

III – 'Samit' Earth

Fire	*Samit : Prthivi*	*Smoke : agni*	*Flame : rātrā night*	*Coals : candramā Moon*	*Sparks : Nakṣatra*	*Oblation : rain*	*Result : Food.*
Ś The abode where all creatures are born & experience the results of their past work & which consists of action, its factors & its results	Just as the samit nourishes the fire similarly this world is nourished; it is furnished with the means of enjoyment for a number of living things. On this world in which all the living things (creatures) have their enjoyment. various animals are born in this world. That is why Pṛthvi is called as Samit.	The fire rises from the earth as the Smoke from fire. Both have same abode, same source so both are compare ᵗ.	The flame is produced from the contact of fuel. The night serves the purpose of flame because as the flame is originated from the fuel added to the fire, so also the night has connection with its fuel (earth) for origination. The shadow of the darkness.	The Moon is called as coal because of the similarity of origin just as coal is produced from flame in the same way moon is produced in the night, or both are same in extinguishable they are compared.	The sparks produced from the coal here the nakṣtras look as if they scatter away in the sky.	In this metaphor the rain is offered as the oblation.	Food is produced out of the oblation.
R	The Pṛthvi is called the samit.	The smoke has connection with the fire, it is produced out of the fuel, in the		not explained	not explained he drops the interpretations of both the constituents.		
The earth			Just as the flame is controlled by the brightness of				

Fire	*Samit : Prthivi*	*Smoke : agni*	*Flame : rātri night*	*Coals : candramā Moon*	*Sparks : Nakṣatra*	*Oblation : rain*	*Result : Food.*
which is spread away till oceans and mountains		the fuel, in the same way, the is related to the Samit (earth).	the brightness of the fire, similarly the night is controlled by the movement of Sun that is why the night is called arci.				
V	'year'	'Sky'	'Night'	'diśa'	'avāntaradiśa'	'varṣa'	'food'

IV—Puruṣa

Fire Puruṣa	*Smit (fuel) : Open Mouth*	*Smoke : Prāṇa*	*Flame : Speech*	*Coals : Eyes*	*Sparks : Ears*	*Oblation : Food*	*Result :*
Ś—Puruṣa should be taken in sense of a man, having organs like head, hands etc.	The open mouth is considered as the fuel in case of the man because through mouth man is lighted up i.e. enlightened with regard to speech, Ś gives a example from the practical life, when a fuel is added in the fire, the fire becomes more lusturous, the flames go higher and higher.	Between the smoke and Prāṇa there is sameness in rising upwards. Both rises from samit, both have the same source.	The speech or the word signifies its object that is why they re compared.	Both represent a pacified state or both are the sources of light; hence they are compared.	Both have the similarity of scattering' so the ears are called the sparks.	In this metaphor the 'food' is offered as the oblation.	Retas
Rg— He never explains the word Puruṣa	not explained	—	He understands 'vāc' having the quality to illumination.	Other two are not explained by him.			
V different Upaniṣadic texts.	'vāc' Speech	'Prāṇa' Prāṇa	'Jihvā' Tonque	'cakṣu' Eyes	'Śrotra' Ears	'varṣa' Year (similar oblation)	'annam' Food.

V—Yoṣa (Woman)

Fire Yoṣa	*Fuel : Sexual Organ*	*Smoke : Loma*	*Flame : Wagins*	*Coals : Pent-tration*	*Sparks : Rap-ture*	*Oblation : Retas*	*Result :*
Ś	The woman is lighted because of Upasṭha.	Having the same place of origination; both are compared.	Both have similarity in colour.	—	Both have likeness of having existence for a very short time.	In this metaphor the Retas is offered as the oblation	Puruṣa is produced out of this oblation.
Rg	Ś and Rg are identical in explanation.	Both have similarity in having same colour.			The sparks are compared with the abhi-nanda Sukha-lova because both re least concerned.		
V	Sexual Organ.	Confabulation	Vagina	Penetration	Raptures	Retaḥ	Garbha.

SECTION A

BRU 1.3.28.

Ś—The prastotṛ recites the sāmans. The mantra viz., "tamaso mā jyotirgamaya" etc. is repeated at the time of recitation when the prastotr begins to chant the Sāman. These mantras are repeated and this repetition of the mantras is to be done by the sacrificer.

M—He prefers to take these three different prayers and not three distinct mantras. This is the prayer for the removal of the obstacles to the divine world, it produces the best reward.

The phrase viz. "Asato mā sadgamaya" is explained by both the ācāryas differently as follow:—

Ś—It means from the evil actions and ignorance lead me to actions and thoughts, that are regulated by the Scriptures. That is to say the phrase indicate-through the request to help the recitor of the mantra for identifying himself with those objects which lead to the immortality or the divinity. The prayer conveys the thought of making while interpreting i.e. evil means death, that is natural actions and thoughts. Hg—He does not explain.

M—He takes " asat" as death or sorrow and sat means bliss or immortality. The phrase denotes the meaning as follow:—

"from sorrow lead me to the bliss" i.e. it conveys the same meaning following the Ś s explanation viz. " make me immortal.

(2) Tamaso mā jyotir gamaya--

Ś—The word tamas means darkness, death or all ignorance. It has the nature of a veil. Darkness also means the death, being the cause of it.

The vocable jyotir means the light, the immortality. It is one's divine nature. Since the knowledge being the luminous, is called the light; therefore, the knowledge denotes the immortality. Knowledge is of an imperishable nature according to Ś. So the phrase denotes to help one for realising the divine entity. Thus it means to make him the immortal.

Rg—he does not explain.

M— The vocable tamas means the ignorance or the death and "jyoti" renders the meaning as the knowledge or immortality. So the prayer denotes to lead the recitor to the knowledge from the ignorance.

(3) "Mṛtyor mā amṛtam gamaya."

Ś—He interpretes the phrase in a simple way viz., to lead to mukti from the death. He tells that "mṛtyoḥ amṛtam kuru" means to make free from saṁsāra; that amṛtatva is nothing but to becoming free from the saṁsāra according to R.]

M—"mrtyu" means the death; and amṛta means mokṣa according to M. Thus it means "from bondage lead to the mukti.

In all to survey, Ś explains the first mantra denoting to help the prayee to identify himsilf with the objects of realisation instead of those which are not true as such. while the second mantra means, to help him to go beyond that because it is the form of the ignorance and attain the salvation. The third mantra should be taken literally.

M—He disagrees with Ś in the explanation of the some of the words. (1) The vocable 'asat' is not ignorance but it means the "sorrow" according to M's view. So it is called the death. (2) "Sat" is bliss, it is called the immortality (3) "Tamas" is the ignorance in its very nature. So also it is called the death. (4) "Jyotir" is the knowledge naturally it is of the immortal nature. (5) Mṛta is the ordinary death and that can be overcome through the is mokṣa. A mukta is never born under the law of the existence.

Ś—Then after chanting for the sacrifice with the three mantras, the chanter of a mantra should secure eatables for himself by chanting. The chanter is able to obtain the desired object, he is the knower of the vital force.

M—He propounds that the person who knows and meditates with respect on the Vāyu (Prāṇa) called as the Sāman is sure to get the desired world.

M contradicts with Ś and holds a view that Ś inter pretation is not proper. He further argues that of Ś explanation is accepted then the japa of this mantra would be devoid of the fruits. M explains the words mṛtya and amṛta as denoting the well-known meaning viz. The death and the mokṣa respectively. And so they do not require explanation as Ś adds to them. The Śruti has not explained them and M following the Brāhmaṇa sentence viz. "na atra tirohitam iva asati", says the words are very clear and therefore they should not be explained.

M further tells that the Śruti suggests the meaning as- one who knows the meaning of these three prayers viz. asato mā etc. The Śruti does not convey the meaning which Ś explains viz. One who knows the mystery of the Prāṇa because a true udgītha is always a manifestation of the Prāṇa.

BRU 4.3.1

I. Sa mene na vadiṣya...

Ś— Yājñavalkya approached Janaka to see Yogakṣema i.e. to inquire about the welfare of the king janaka. While going there he thought that he should not speak about cosmos.

Rg—He agrees with the Ś's comments.

M—He does not follow Ś and R and observes that Yājñavalkya went to Janaka wishing to hold a conversation and to discuss with him.

S. Radhakrishnan comments on M's view that if the line is read "sam enena vadiṣya iti" ("came to Janaka intending to speak with him") it is only an ingenious conjecture.[1]

Formerly when Janaka Vaideha and Yājñavalkya had held a discussion on Agnihotra, Yājñavalkya had granted him a boon. Janaka choose the right to ask any question when he desired; therking, therefore, starts putting questions.

II. किं ज्योति ? कतम आत्मा ?

The words "किं ज्योति" and "कतम आत्मा" refers to the self or Brahman according to *Ś* and *R*. The Self is the light different from one's body and organs and illumines them though it is itself not illuminated by anything else. The self is present in all the states of waking, dream and deep sleep.

M—The question proposed by Janaka is about the innermost light in man.

V—BRU 4.3.2 refers to the nature of puruṣa for the first time in the Ups.

III. BRU 4.3.7

कतम आत्म्येति योऽयं विज्ञानमयः प्राणेषु.....

लोकमति क्रामति मृत्यो रूपाणिः।

Ś—The Up. answers the nature of the Self (Ātman). "Vijñānamaya" means intellect. The Self is perceived as inhaving contact with the intellect just as a night is associated with the Sun and the Moon. The intellect helps in every king of knowledge. It serves the prupose of the lamp in darkness.[2] Ś. cites the Śruti.

It is through the mind that one sees and hears. The objects are lighted up by a lamp in the darkness. Every object is perceived because of its association with intellect.

Ś criticises those who explain the word "Vijñānamaya" as a modification of the consciousness i.e. to say this explanation goes against the Śruti. According to Ś the suffix mayat in the word "Vijñānamaya" denotes something else than modification. The Self stays in the heart; it illumines the body and organs with its own intelligence.[3] The examples from BG. are quoted to prove that the Self is light within intellect; infinite, all pervading like the ether. The self is self-effulgent.

The Self effulgent light pervades the intellect; the Self assumes the likeness of the intellect and seems to think (dhyāyatīva) just as the light locks coloured. The Self seems to become whatever the intellect resembles it. So When the intellect turns into a dream, the Self also assumes that form.

Ś argues that it is only the likeness of the intellect that gives rise to the delusion that the Self moves between the two worlds and has such other activities.

The words "mṛtyorupāṇi" in the Śruti are explained as the forms of death referring to work, ignorance and death has no other forms of its own.

Ṛg— He explains and discusses the Śruti with the help of BG and BRS.

M—He takes the word Ātman (Self) referring to the Lord Bhagavati. The Ātman is alone the light of the man. To strengthen his point he cites the quotations from the Skanda Purāṇa.[4] Ātmā is the great light and guide. According to M, the Ātmic light does not mean the light of one's own Self but the light supreme. He further explains that the Ātman is the Supreme one, all knowledge who lives in the heart. He remain steady and makes the Jīva to do activities. He quotes the Mahamimāṁsa to illustrate the Ātman more promptly.

The terms 'dhyāyativa' 'lelāyativa' means "grasps" according to M. And The word Vijnanamayā is taken in the sense of "all knowledge". He produces the changes in the

Jiva. Her causes the Jīva to travel in both the worlds. He is called "स हि स्थानो भूत्वा" (Saṁ hi svapno bhūtvā) because he is responsible for creating the dreams in the dream state.

Ś—The phrase "Imam Lokaṃ" means the state of consciousness. It is called "forms of death" because it causes to commit all sorts of the sins and the sin is nothing but death.

"svapno bhātvā" means He becomes the carrier of the soul to antarikṣa or dream world after death. In this world the jīvas are subject to death, so it is "mṛtyorupāṇi".

M—He interpretes the word "imaṁ lokaṁ" as a synonymous of the waking state in the same way, The word 'heaven' (Svarga) as Suṣupti and aṅtarikṣa as a dream condition. M. adds two meanings to the word 'lokau' in the 'ubhau lokau" i.e. (1) Worlds (2) States of consciousness.

Ś— refutes Yogācāra school of the Buddhist in the Śruti by the words 'एवं स्थाने भवतः'; – According to the Buddhist, the above quoted phrase refers to the two abodes, i.e. this and the next world.

IV. BRU 4.3.8—"स वा अयं पुरुषो जायमानः...."

The dream state is a junction between the waking condition and the deep sleep. In it one feels joys and sufferings, which consist the impressions of the experiences of the previous lives. On the other hand the glimpses of the rewards of the merits and the demerits, those are to be happen in the future life are experienced through the urge of those merits and demerits, or through the grace of the god.

Ś—He supposes that one sees many objects in the dreams those are not experienced in this life.

Ṛg—According to him one sees this world in the dream; or sometimes the person sees the other world viz. svarga, naraka, in the dream. That is why the dream condition is "vilakṣaṇa", in which one experiences the objects from two worlds.

M—According to M The Śruti refers to (1) Lord (2) Jīva. M shows distinction between the Jīva and the Īśvara. M. wants to prove that the condition of suṣupti and death are the same with the help of BRS 1.3.42.[5]

Actually there is no need to take the help of the Vedānta Sūtra in this portion. The BRU is the earlier work though M quotes Vedānta Sūtras for explaining his views without the necessity.

The doctrine set forth by the Yājñavalkya has a prominent place among the various philosophical schools. On this particular passage Ś, R, M builds up theories and developed their views.

V. BRU 4.3.10

"न तत्र रथा न रथयोगा...सृजन सहि कर्ता"

Ś—Ś states that He himself creates the objects like the chariot, animals, roads etc. Really there are neither objects nor activities of the organs exist in the dream state, but their impressions are visible. In the dream condition the self becomes distinct altogether.He is Himself the light. One dreams only when the organs have ceased to function. Therefore no other light (than the Self) can exist in that state. Moreover the dream state cannot be supposed as the waking-state. In the waking-state the self is engaged in many objects; it is mixed up with the living objects.

Ṛg—He states that the objects like chariots, ways wells etc. which are experienced in the dream could not seen in the waking condition but those objects are created by the Paramātman.

He argues that the objects seen in the dream is not seen

in the same form in the waking-state. Moreover their marks of presence or their marks of destruction are not available and the objects which are visible in the dream-state, are created by the Paramātman.

M—The Śruti is explained according to his principle by M. i. e. the world is the real, and he contradicts with the non-dualism-the point viz. The world is unreal. M. denotes the Vedānta Sūtra[6] for making his arguements solid. M. refutes Ś on the ground of the differnce between the waking state and the dream state. The objects perceived in the dream-state by a person exist in the world really. The unseen objects are not seen in the dream. M. criticises that the pleasures and pains created by the objects are not false or unreal but they are real, since one experiences them in whatever state. Ś takes the world as unreal because a stage comes when one realises that in the past the world was not existing; the world does not come into existence in the future.

According to the Ś the agency attributed to the self is only figurative. The light of the Self which is pure intelligence, illumines the body and the organs and thus they perform their functions being illumined by Him.

According to *Ṛg* the agent is the Supreme Lord.[7] The self is unattached in the dream-state because the effects produced form the contact of the objects, are not found in it.

M—Supposes that the Keśava performs all the activities. He is not seen by Jīva even at the time of the death of the dreaming-state. M. does not recognise the dream-state as the separate one. M states that the lord is always the light of the Jīva even in the waking-state. The lord is independent and he is seen by the Muktas only.

Ś— does not regard the dream condition and the death as one condition. The self transcends the forms of the death and not death itself. In dream though the Self is separated from the body and the organs it experiences joy, fear etc. However the death is not the nature of the self. The self is unattached in the dream-state because the effects produced from the contact of the objects, are not found to it. The Self in the sound sleep gets the highest serenity. While in the waking state a man gets impurities due to the mixture of the innumerable activities of the body.

The Self makes the body to sleep but the Self remains awake and notices the impressions of the deeds, that have been left upon the mind. The self causes the body to awake. In sleep condition there is respite from the craving and the aversions, fear and anxieties. In it the individual is absolutely one with the divine one.

VI. BRU 4.3.15,16,17.

The Up. establishes that the self is Itself the light and distinct from the body organs and their stimulating causes desire, work, on account of its non-attachment. It is unattached because it moves by turn from the waking to the dream state, from this to the deep sleep, then again to the dream, then to the waking-state; Thus the Self is distinct from the three-states. The example of a fish is given for the support of this point i.e. just as a fish moves freely to both the banks of a river, similarly the Self moves to both these states.

Ś—Ś takes the Self as eternal, free is superimposed by the ignorance. The person fancies himself in good or bad position due to the impressions on the created by ignorance, viz. The person has a dream that the robber comes and goes to kill him. Actually nobody is going to kill him. Here the impressions are falsely manifested. when the ignorance goes away and the knowledge reaches its perfection, the identity with the Self is attained. Ignorance presents the things other than the self those are non-existent, and makes the Self as limited. Then the desire arises for that from which he is separated that desire prompts him to do the action which produces the result. Ignorance is not a natural characteristic of the self, because it automatically dicreases as the knowledge increases and when the knowledge is at its highest level, ignorance disapperars completely.

M—He explains the vocable and avidyā differently from Ś. M supposes that the word 'avidyā' is a compound (आ+विद्या)' 'आ' (ā) refers to the Viṣṇu and the vidyā means the knowledge. So M interpretes the word avidyā thus-the knowledge obtained through Viṣṇu is 'avidya'.

And this avidyā causes to have dreams in the dream-condition of to perceive the objects in the waking condition.

M supposes the Self as no other but the lord Viṣṇu; and he is eternal, fearless, free from all the sins. There is no other than Him. That thing exists which is seen by the Lord Viṣṇu. The gods like Brahmā and other see the objects due to the favour or the Viṣṇu, They are not independent seers.

VIII. BRU 4.3.32.

सलिल एको द्रष्टाऽद्वैतो भवत्येष...........

Ś—The state in which one sees nothing else; hears nothing else, knows nothing else, is the highest of all the attainments. It reveals the identification with all.

"This is its supreme glory" (Paramā gati):—It is the highest of all the splendours and it is not attached artificially to it; it is its own nature. Other glories are artificial.

"This is his highest world":— The other worlds which are the effects of its past work, are inferior to it. This world cannot be secured by any action.

"This is his Supreme bliss":—This bliss is eternal; the other pleasures and delights, which are rewards of the enjoyments, are produced from the contact of the organs

with various objects. Therefore they are momentary; but this highest bliss is everlasing, so the BRU 4.3.32 says others live on a particle of this highest bliss.

Ś takes the literal meanings to the words like man, god, emperors, gandharvas, prajāpati etc. and the world of Brahman is taken in the sense of Hiraṇya garbha.

Ṛg—He propounds that the Jīva becomes one with Paramātman, but the Jīva is not completely merged with Brahman. The Brahman and the Jīva are not one. On the contrary the Jīva are many due to the association with the Prajnātman. The Jīva is very pure, devoid of any doṣa like the water, and just as a drop of water added in the water becomes one with it. Similarly the Jīva goes to Brahman. There is no complete identification between the Jīva and the Brahman. Herein R differs from Ś's docrtrine viz. Jīva and Brahman are the same. while according to R Jīva is the part of Paramātman. There is no identification R further teaches that the difference between the devas etc. goes away.

Ṛg states that in this condition the objects which have difference, and their knowledge due to their contacts with the sense organs, and their relation with the merits; all of them are not seen. Thus only no other entity is experienced and this is the highest gati. R takes the meaning of Paramā gatih differently viz. the gatiḥ which is obtained through the arcīr-mārga by the Jīva. This is the highest wealth. R takes this phrase in the sense, the wealth which is obtained by the tattvajnānins. *This the highest world*—Means this is the immutable place for enjoyment according to the view of R. *This is the highest bliss*— Which is unsurpassed and favourable.

M—M refutes the principle set forth by ś with the arguement; scriptures do not prove the world as unreal or the perception of the world is a wrong notion on the mind of a jiva produced by the error. With the help of Gītā[8], M emphsises on the point that the scriptures follow his view by mentioning "those persons who think the world to be false, they are called Asuras."

M refers to the sensations like the taste, the smell, the touch and the functions like the thinking, the hearing; the touching etc. for proving the point that there is the distinction between the Lord and the world. M splits the words in two ways :— (1) referring to the Lord;

(2) referring to the world.

According to M the highest entity is one alone, (ekaḥ advitiyaḥ); without second ; He exists at the time of the dissolution. Prakṛti pervades the whole universe in the form of the water and no other living being exists at the time of dissolution. The epithet in the Śruti viz. "Brahmaloke" means the perfect knowledge. The term 'Brahma' means 'perfect' and loka is knowledge in the vocable "brahmaloka".

Jīva enters into the heart at the time of the death. Then he perceives the Lord Viṣṇu only, which dwells in the heart. Jīva depends on the Lord and becomes unconsciousness. The Jiva does not cognise anything else. The Viṣṇu shines out with his own glory and illumines the upper part of the heart and the lord goes out through this passage. He takes him and Prāṇa along with. The other devas (lower Prāṇas) follow this chief Prāṇa; Vidyā; Karma are also with them. Vidyā, Karma, Yogyatā are taken to be referring to the several devatas of those names, i.e. Garuḍa is presiding deity of the knowledge etc. All of them follow the Viṣṇu when He goes out of the body at the time of the Mukta's death. Mukta leaves the body through Suṣumṇā nāḍi. The Lord throws away the body of the Jīva and takes the hold of the subtle from the Jīva; just as a leech takes the hold of the another blade of the grass before quitting the grass on which it is moving.

The lord creates now body of a Jīva according to his merit just as a goldsmith destroyes the impurity of the gold, He gives the knowledge to the Jīva by removing avidyā. The Jīvas get the body accordingly to which class they belong i.e. to say if the Jīva belongs to the class of the Pitṛs. He creates Pitṛs body and so on. The released soul reaches to Lord Hari and acquires the quantity of the bliss.

M supposes that all the Jīvas have true existence. In fact Lord and Jīva are distinct from each other. Since no one sees that the Jīva is the all-knowing one as the Lord is. The Jīva has little powers. It is not present every where.

Śankarānanda on Paryaṅkavidyā

Āruṇi ordered his son to handle the priest-hood of the Citra Gargyāṇi king. When Śvetaketu went to the assembly of the Citra, he was well received. At that time, the king asked a question that what will be the fruit of the sacrifice i.e. if the king would go to the heaven or would be tied down to the earth. Śvetaketu could not reply and therefore, he took the king's permission to go back and learn the answer from his father. On his return Śvetaketu put those same questions to the Āruṇi for which Āruṇi confessed his ignorance. Then after Āruṇi decided to learn them from the king himself. Both of them went to the king's assembly. Āruṇi with the sacrificial twigs in his hand as a token of accepting his apprenticeship went there. The king Citra was pleased with him for his very act, refined behaviour, and the king praised the Āruṇi and promised him to explain the mystery. The king fully expounds the vidyā as follow :—

In the beginning it is told that all the departed souls go to the region of the Moon to reap the fruit of their deeds.

KAU directly mentions the paths by which the souls travel i.e. if one dies in the bright half of the month, he goes beyond the region of the Moon but if anyone dies in the dark half, he is thrown down to the earth through the rains to be born as a reptile, serpant, mosquito or any other animal Therefore the moon is said to be the entrance to the heaven. It can be said with this context that the Moon is the check post for the onward journey of a soul.

The KAU 1.1 expressly refers to Devayāna path though both the paths viz the Devayāna and the pitṛyāna are mentioned as leading for the other world. When one ascends up, he reaches the region of Brahmā by stages. First he enters to the region of the fire god, then to the air god; then to the sun-god; then to the Varuṇa; to the Indra and to the Prajāpati; step by step, and ultimately to the region of the Brahmā. The world of Brahmā is full of the tanks; the rivers; the trees; the cities; the palaces protected by the Indra and the Prajāpati. The descriptions of the Brahmā's world is figurative. There is the Brahmā's hall where the intelligence is the throne and also couch of the incomparable splendour. The favourite is imaginary which the scholars take to be the nature (matter) and the reflection is visual. The scriptures and the understanding are considered as the nymphs. At the command of the Brahmā five hundred nymphs go to welcome him at once. Then he if being the knower of Brahmā, then adorned in Brahmic form, goes to Brahmā. He crosses the pond made of the cupidity and the anger if any ignorant soul reaches the pond he falls into it.

S.K. Belvalkar and R.D. Ranade opine that the chapter of the KAU starts the discussion between the king Citra Gārgyāyāṇi and the Śvetaketu by which the soul's progress towards the world of the Brahmā is explained. According to him the world of the Brahmā is the highest goal and a true place of the safety. A departed soul travels by the two paths leading to the another world; these two paths run up together upto the world of the Moon, and then divert into the two directions i.e. the upward and the downward. Belvalkar summarises the Upaniṣadic passage.

According to the view of the Deussen all the souls that depart from this world reach to the Moon first. The vital breaths of the soul are responsible for the waxing and the waning of the Moon. i.e. it is said,"through their life, the waxing lunar half (of the month) grows and by the virtue of its, wanning half, it conveys them to the rebirths."The Moon is the door of the higher region. There the soul's knowledge is tasted, if he is able to answer goes by the Devayāna path. The Devayāna path stands in higher degree than the Moon and if the ascending soul does not pass in the test, he goes to the Pitṛyāna path. That means the Moon is the responsible entity who allows the departed soul to become the rain etc. and to rain down below. It seems that the Deussen wants to emphasis that the departed soul whether it may be the doer of the good deed or the evil deeds reach the Moon by one and the same way. From the Moon the path diverts. On the other hand the CHU and the BRU describes in the state way that a person who acts in good manner or performs the tapas or the sacrifice etc. Obtains the fruit of the good deeds and he goes by the Devayāna, while the other person goes by the Pitṛyāna.

Śaṅkarānanda on KAU 3.1

The KAU 3.1 starts expounding the knowledge through a discourse between the Pratardana and the Indra. Pratardana went to the abode of Indra by means of prowess and his heroic struggles. Indra was so much pleased with him that he wanted to grant a boon to be chosen by Pratardana. But Pratardana left it to the choice of Indra. Indra refuses to do so by stating that a superior has no right to choose for inferior and he asked to select it to the Pratardana. At that time Pratardana refuses and forces Indra to give knowledge which is wholesome to the mankind. Indra then propounded him the mystery and imparted "know Himself" who is the truth. Indra preached the self. Indra further preached that the vital air is the life and it is the self. There is life in the animals because the bodily organs and the breath functions cooperatively. It is the consciousness of 'self' in the every act of perception which is again the function of the human brain. It is the introspection. The life persists as long as the vital air is present in the body. The vital air works uniformly with the organs. That is why one sees forms with the eyes, hears sounds with the ears etc. The life force with the vital breath which is stated in the Up. is the "Self" or 'Brahman. And the worship of this self leads to the immortality.

The vital breath controls the functioning of the organs. One can live without the tongue or the sight etc. but without the vital breath the life is impossible.The bodily organs do not discharge their respective functions without the co-operation of the vital breath. The functions of organs merge into the vital breath, while one is asleep or in a swoon. All the organs are active due to its existence in the body and stop to discharge their respective functions when the vital breath ceases to act. This vital breath or the Prāṇa is superior over all the sensory and the motor organs. According to the medical science the vital breath is the action of lungs, depending on the action of the heart.

Then the function of the brain or the nervous system under the term 'Prajñā' is described. The functions of the organs depend in the nervous system. All the bodily organs discharge their functions by intelligence viz. the speech without the intelligence do not convey any meaning. The activity of a person depends upon the mind i.e. to say sometimes a person engrossed in the work does not notice the sound of the clock. There are three factors in a cognition of the object : (1) the perceiver, the perceived object and the act of perception. The act of perception is done by the help of intelligence which is called as 'Prajñā' in the Up. The 'Prajñā' is identified with the vital breath and it is all in all; end in all. It is the lord of the universe. Indra goes on to identify viz. "It is myself"; it is yourself". It is the supreme soul.

The KAU 3.1 expounds the term Prāṇa in the co-relation of Prajñā very excellently. It shows how the sense organs and the motor organs depend on each other for their respective work from the point of the modern science also. Therefore Deussen agrees with 'KAU follows well ordered and excellently presented consideration based on the essentially right psychological view about the dependence of the sense-objects on the sense organs and of these sense organs on the Prāṇa or "Prajñātman".[10]

The Prāṇa and the 'Prajñātman' are explained as identical because they live together in the body and go out of it togetherly. Thus Prāṇa+Prajñā=Ātman. It does not increase or discrease on the effect of good or bad deeds. This is the Indra (Ātman) which one should know.

MAU with Rāmatirtha's Commentary

The discourse between the king Bṛhadratha and a the sage Śākāyanya which deals with Brahmavidyā. The king was totally fade up with the world and so decided to go in the forest to perform the tapas. After some days the sage called Śākāyanya was pleased with the king and asked him to select a boon. The king wished to know the Ātman's knowledge, Śākāyanya stressed on the view that the king's request was very difficult to attain. The Brahmavidyā is not easily learnt and so advised the king to ask for some worldly pleasures, worldly enjoyments did not give bliss. They are not satisfied but on the other hand they increased day by day because they are connected with the cupidity, anger, greed, delusion, fear etc. Thus they are transient and perishable, so the king considered them useless. This frame of the king's mind moved the sage to consider him as a worthy person for imparting the Ātman's knowledge. The speech of the king shows his mental capacity and the earnest desire to know the 'self'.

Śākāyanya thereafter explained the 'Self' as Śuddhaḥ Putaḥ Śāntoprāno niratmantokṣayaḥ Stiraḥ-aśāśavathḥ etc. In the human body there is one subtle substance which is intelligent, incomprehensible and invisible. This self stimulates the body to act.

The body is compared with a chariot, the motor organs with the horses, the sensory organs with the reins, the mind with the driver and the inborn nature with the whip. The body goes round like a wheel. In this way the body moves and appears intelligent. The self is the mover of it.

REFERENCES

1. Deussen Paul, "Sixty Upanishads of the Veda" (Tran. by Bedekar, V.M. and Palsule, G.B.), Vol. I, p.140.
2. Kansara, N.A.,'Sambodhi' Vol. 10, p.43, ft.
1. Radhakrishnan, S., vide The principal Upanishads, BRU., p. 255.
2. of. BRU i. 4.3.
3. BG. 13.33. As the Sun illumines the whole world, so the Self, the owner of the rield of this body illumines the body.
4. vide BRU with Madhava's commentary. SBH. series, Vol. XIV, p. 436.
5. BRS 1.3.42, "Suṣuptyukrāntyo bheden".
6. op. cit. Deussen Paul,"The Sixty upanishads of the Veda" (translated by Bedekar, V.M. and Palsule, G.B.), Vol. I, p.25.

SECTION B

Upaniṣads and Brahma-Sūtras

(BRS) 3.3.6

The BRU 1.3.7 is discussed in the BRS 3.3.6 in which it is showed that some vidyās are different though they apparently look similar.

The BRU 1.3.7 is discussed with the CHU 1.2.7; the subject matter of which is the worship of the Prāṇa.

Ś (788-820 A.D.) He takes the two vidyās separately becaue the subject matter differs in both the Śrutis. In the CHU 1.2.7 it is stated that only the part of the Udgītha viz 'aum' is to be meditated on as the Prāṇa, while in the BRU 1.3.7 the entire Udgītha viz. 'aum' is to be meditated on as the Prāṇa, so both the vidyās enjoined by the Śrutis are different.

R (1017-1127 A.D.) He agrees with Ś since both the vidyās are regarded as different.

M (1197-1273 A.D.) He does not follow the Ś, R'S view while interpreting the Sūtras. He holds the view that this adhikaraṇa establishes the contemplation of the Supreme. Being with all the attributes having the equal importance though the attributes may be positive or negative.

V—(1479-1531 A.D.) He does not refer.

N—(Later half of 15th century) He follows R's interpretation.

(2) BRU 4.3.2-5 Katama ātma iti...is referred in the sūtra kartā Śastrārtharvālt (BRU 2.3.33). The Sutra discusses the nature of the self.

Ś—He takes the Śruti as referring to the Brahman and to the Jīva. Jīva has no powers to play himself according to Ś.

R— He refers these Śrutis in the BRS 2.3.33 also. The topic of the Sūtra is the 'Self'. He describes the Ātman as 'हृत्कमल मध्यगश्च प्राण शाब्दिनेन्द्रिय मध्यगे विज्ञान धर्मक:' The order of the words in the text of the tika by Ṛg. instead of "कतम आत्मा इति" as given in the Upanisadic text and this B text.

M—He interpretes this Sūtra in a different way. The Sūtra deals with the kartṛtva, it is attributed to the Jīva, if the jīva is accepted as the doer then only the injunctions lead by the scriptures prove to be true otherwise all the Śāstras would be invalid. The Sūtra therefore, emphasises the jiva as the agent in his own accord with certain limits. According to the view of M the injunctions and the prohibitions of the Śāstras apply to the agent in the person of the jīvas. They can not apply to the supreme self because if they are considered as referring to the self, the self will be liable to merit and demerit and thereby will lose his higher status. Thus the agency of the Jīva has to be accepted in order to preserve the meanigfulness of the injunctions and prohibitions of the scriptures.

M disagrees with the Ś, R views and he concludes that this adhikaraṇa resolves the conflict of testimony regarding the self's agency. The conflict is seen between the texts like BRU. 4.4.5, which refers to the self, reaping the fruits of its actions and others which consider the supreme self, the sole agent; that there is in the world.

V—He quotes the Śruti in the same sūtra and explains that it is asked for the first time that what is the nature of the Puruṣa in the Ups. According to V, it seems that the Śruti states two objects viz. (1) Jīva because Jīva is the Brahman as Ups. describe while on the other hand it refers (2) To the Brahman since it states the root "jñā" as its object.V supposes that the Brahman is the object of the knowledge and It shines in the heart and the body, though jīva and Brahma are similar to each other partly; but the actions of the jīva and Brahman are similar to each other partly; but the actions of the Jīva depends on the Brahman. The jīva has no powers to play himself.

N—He does not refer this Śruti in this Sūtra.

(3) BRU 4.3.7 "Katama Ātma....hṛdyantarjyotiḥ" is discussed in the BRS 2.3.42 and 43 for the second time.

The "Suṣuptyutrāntyadhikaraṇam" has a subject from this Śruti. It is as follwo: The word Vijñānamyat (he who consists of the knowledge) referred to, is the Brahman and not the individual soual. In the condition of the deep sleep and with reference to the departure of it from the body; the individual soul and the Highest soul are spoken as different from each other. since the śruti viz BRU 4.4.22 uses the words like Vāśi, iśānaḥ, adhipati etc.

Ś-Ś takes these two sūtras viz. BRS 2.3.42 and 43 as the beginning of a new topic, while R takes the three sūtras viz. 41-43 as a one section dealing with the question sūtras viz. 41-43 as a one section dealing with the question whether the ether in the CHU 8.14 refers to the Brahman or the indvidual soul. According to Ś the adhikaraṇa deals with state of the deep sleep and the going out of it from the body at the time death. The sūtra 42 points out the difference of the highest soul and the invidivual soul in the states of the deep sleep and the time of death. The śrūti refers to the Highest self only according to the view of Ś because the beginning and the end of the chapter deals with one topic always. Ś quotes BRU 4.3.14-22 for strengthening his view. Further he argues that the description of the nature the embodied self does not lead to the highest achievement. So the topic is regarding the difference of the Highest self from such conditions.

R—the śrutis are quoted as a reply to the objector's point. R supposes that the Paramātman is a different entity from the Pratyagātman who goes to the Paramātman in the deep sleep condition and who leaves the body at the time of Utkrānti. Therefore the goer and the one gone to must be distinct. R cities BRU 4.3.7 to introduce the view that the Paramānti. R cities BRU 4.3.7 to introduce the view that the Paramātman and the Jīvātman both are not identical. Similarly R quotes the other two śrutis viz. (1) BRU 4.3.21 (2) BRU 4.3.35 to show the Paramātman different from the Jīva.

M—BRU 4.3.9 is quoted in the BRS 2.2.3.9 for the refutation of Ś's doctrine. M strongly opposed to the principle of Ś i.e. jīva is not a doer (Karta). M feels that the Kartṛtva should be attached to the jiva because the scriptures enjoins varioius Yāgas like jyotiṣtoma etc. To the Jīva. He feels that if a person does not perform the enjoined work then he would without getting its reward and then the scriptures would be useless.

So according to the V Jīva is a doer of the actions but it does not have the power of Brahma that is why he does ahita-karma. jīva has two powers (1) prakriyā Śakti and (2) Jñāna-Śakti. That is the Kartṛtva of jīva is natural.

V—He supposes that the Jīva and the Brahman are distinct to some. extent. one is happy and the other is un-happy. The two conditions viz. Suṣupti and Utkrānti show the variant and nature of the Jīva and the Brahman. The Lord himself makes him to go to the other world. The Utrānki is not a natural act ot the Jīva.The acts done in the dream condition are unreal. In waking condition also the असंगत्व ज्ञान is told with reference to the Jīva. V gives the example of the fish i.e. to say though the fish lives in the river; both the river and the fish are not the same all the time. Similarly jīva acts in the waking and the dreaming state. The knowledge that is produced vary from one another. The fish moves on the both banks of the river for having no attachment for that place. in the same way Jīva has no attachment for both the conditions. In suṣ upti jīva gets Brahman means his actions are ceased. It may be observed that the Śrutis are splitted acording to V's principles.

N—He quotes BRU 4.3.7 "Yoyam vijnanamaya... Pranesu etc. in the different adhikaraṇa as different from the other ācāryas. BRS 2.3.2[2]

Ś—The Śruti is quoted for declaring the objector's view i.e. The soul is not atomic because the Śruti mentions the greatness. N takes the topic of the Śruti distinct from the objector. The subject of it is about the supreme soul. N also quotes the BRU 4.3.7 in the BRS 2.3.7 in the BRS 2.3.24 to prove that the soul is of the atomic size. He abides in one part of the body i.e. in the heart (hṛdyantajyotir).

In BRS 2.3.21 the Śruti of the BRU 4.3.7 is taken for referring to the supreme soul. How in BRS 2.3.24 N mentions the abode of the Jīva with the help of the same Śruti.

(4) BRU 4.3.9.10

"Na tatra rathā rathyogā panthānaḥ...sa hi kartā." The Śrutis are quoted in BRS 3.2.1.[3]

The adhikaraṇa deals with the cognition in the dream. The dream condition is an intermediate state between the waking and the deep sleep.

Ś—According to Ś the topic of this adhikaraṇa is whether the dream condition is real or it is unreal. The opponent takes this Śruti in support of his view. i.e. The objects created in dream condition are real as those of the waking state since the Śruti BRU 4.3.10 tell that "He creates tanks, lotus pools rivers etc. Ś contradicts with the objector's view by arguing that the objects perceived in the dream condition are not real because they are not bound by rules of the space, time etc. viz. one may have a dream that he is walking on the road in the summer's afternoon though he sleeps in winter's night. Similarly the materials for creating the objects are not found in a dream state. Moreover the objects in the dreams are sublated every day when he wakes up. So the dream condition is a mere cognition. Further Ś states that sometimes the drems are prophetic of the future good of bad; may be real just as the appearance of silver in pearl oyster is false yet it produces the joy in us.

Moreover Ś emphasises that because the individual soul is the part of the Brahman. he produces the objects like chariots, rivers etc. only with volition in the dreams; cannot be agreed. The individual soul is hidden like a fire in wood. Its power of creation becomes manifest when the bondage of avidyā is removed through meditation. The soul is a subject of avidyā therefore it cannot be real creator. Therefore all that is cognized in the dream is not real.

R—R also discusses these Śrutis in the BRS 3.2.1. The dream creation is done by the individual soul or by the Lord is the subject matter discussed in this adhikaraṇa. R differs from Ś regarding the adhikaraṇa's topic.

R quotes those śrutis when he discusses on the waking, dream and deep sleep states associated with the individual soul. He tells that the dream creation can be assigned to the Parampuruṣa since it is an extra-ordinary and wondeful creation. Such creation cannot be attributed to the Jīva when the Jīva is not fully manifested in the Saṁsāra. Moreover R thinks the appearance of the objects in the dreams is absolute māyā in the sense that thay are wonderful. Māyā means wonderful power according the view of R. R means to say that the Śruti viz. BRU 4.3.9 emphasises that the objects are not perceived by any other person except the dreaming one.

So the creation of the dreams is attributed to the supreme soul and not to the individual soul, since the nature of the individual soul is hidden owing to the wish of the highest self.

M—He affirms that the dreams are the real and valid experiences. The objects like the chariots, horses, roads which are pereeived in the dream are created by the supreme Being and then after they are withdrawn by the supreme Being himself. Thus M removes the contradiction in the Śruti viz. "There were no chariots, horses or roads there (before). By making such type of arguement M tries to silence Ś's doctrine viz. the objects which are seen in the dream are not real; on the other hand M emphasises his principle with the help of the śruti that the objects which are cognized in the dreams, do come into the existence by the supreme Being and at the same time they are withdrawn after their presentation by the supreme self at his own will. Thus they are not unreal.

M further propounds that the vāsanas or the subtle impressions left by the experience of the past, serve the purpose of the material cause of the dream creations and God's will operates as the efficient cause. The dream creations are not competent to the objects of the waking life because they are due to the gross elements.

V—He mentions the BRS 3.2.1 adhikaraṇa consists of the dream creation as its subject matter. He agrees with Ś on this point.

He does not contradict with Ś on the main point that the various objects like the horse. the road, the chariot which are created in the dream state are unreal. He tells that the objects seen in the dream condition are perceived in the different from the objects which are seen in the waking state. Moreover in the dreaming state there is no consistancy between the two incidences. V criticises on R when he argues the śruti does not insist whether those are real or unreal. Secondly he teaches that the Śruti insists the world as real and not the dreams. V differs from Ś in the explanation of reasons while taking the dream creation as unreal.

N—N takes the subject matter of the adhikaraṇa different from Ś and V. He agrees with R on this point viz. the dream creation is due to the individual soul or the lord, is the topic discussed in this adhikaraṇa.

N supposes that the appearance of the objects in the dream condition must be attributed to the supreme soul alone because such a wonderful creation cannot be made by the individual soul. The attributes of the Jīva are hidden through the wish of the supreme Lord. they are not manifested naturally. Lord Vāsudeava creates the objects in dreams through his own powers, Who is the expert in the act of creating and destroying all wondeful objects.

R and N unnecessarily inteprete this Śruti as involving the discussion about the act of the dream creation belonging to the individual soul or to the supreme soul. The BRU 4.3.10 tries to evaluate the objects in the waking and the dream states. The śruti is mentioned in the context of the subject whether the objects in the waking state and in the dream state are the same or not. Moreover the Śruti differentiates the objects from both the conditions and states that the cognition of the number of the objects in the dreams is distinct from the cognition of the waking condition.

V—V does not put strong and firm statement to criticise Ś' principle i.e.The objects in the dreams do not manifest fully clearly as they are manifested in the waking. They are perceived distinctly.

The difference between the two ācāryas :—viz Ś and V, do not appear much. Both of them emphasis on the same point in some or other way, in different words,V follows the tradition and tries to expound new doctrine with the same ideas. While Ś' interpretation appears more apt and natural citing appropritate and logical reasons to convey his ideas. Ś takes into account the Upaniṣadic cream and remains faithrul to the Śruti more then any other ācāryas.

(5) BRU 4.3.11 is quoted in the BRS 2.3.18 [4].

The adhikaraṇa consists of the discussion regarding the soul's nature i.e. it is nitya or it is anitya. The individual soul is of the nature of intelligence. So the question dealt in the adhikarana is regarding this intelligence, if it is natural to it or it is adventitious .

Ś—He expounds that the intelligence is the very Svarūpa of the Jīva. It is not a quality but it is Brahman Itself. It is manifested as the Jīva because of its contact with the limiting adjuncts. Ś refutes Vaiśeṣikas view i.e. the soul is itself non-intelligence. Ś explains 'jña' as nitya caitanya.

R—He criticises on Ś interpretation of 'jña jña' means Jñātṛ (knower) according to R. R uses this Sūtra to refute the Saṁkhya doctrine and the Advaitins. He argues that the soul is a knowing agent instead of the intelligence. R takes it as the 19th Sūtra instad of 18; where he discusses the size of the individual soul and its residence.

M—M disagrees with all the ācāryas while the interpretation of the Sutra is considered. M argues that the jivatman too has birth from the Brahman. He put forth the reason for his stand point that all the intelligent beings enter into the supreme light of the supreme Being. They are not dissolved into the Brahman. Thus M's doctrine viz the Jīva are seperate from the Brahman is present herein. The Jiva is not merged into the Brahman, while jīva and Brahman both are distinct elements.

V—'jña' denotes the objects as Brahman. Brahman is the object of the knowledge.

N—He follwos R.

BRU 4.3.21.

Prājñenātmanā saṁpariṣvakto na bāhyaṁ kiñcana veda... nāntaram' is quoted in the BRS 1.4.18.

Ś—He anticipates that the Sūtrakāra refers this Śruti to indicate the knowledge about Brahman.

R—He quotes the Śruti in BRS 1.4.18 in Śrī Bhāṣyam. R adopts Ś' view. He attacks on the Saṁkhya theory of Pradhāna.

N—He quotes this Śruti in order to show the difference between the Jīva and the Brahman in the deep sleep and the death.

(6) KATU 1.2.25, is quoted in the BRS 1.2.9-10

The Śruti is a subject matter of the atrudhikaraṇa. The adhikaraṇa discusses the eater of the world. As Ups contradict with each other (MU 3.1.1 and BRU 1.4.6) the confusion is settled about if the eater is fire or the individual soul or the Highest Self.

Ś—He regards the eater as the Highest self since the description of KATU 1.2.25 viz. 'the eater of movable and immovable as his food.' Can be applied to Brahman only because all the elements are created, sustained and reabsorbed in him.

Ś holds this view from the context. Ś referred the KATU 1.2.18.22-23 to prove the Brahman as the eater as mentioned in KATU 1.2.25.

R—He agrees with the interpretation of Ś regarding the adhikaraṇa as whole. According to R eating of carācara with mṛtyu as the appetiser means the withdrawing of the carācara world in him Parmātman. But his adhikaraṇa starts with Sūtra 9 to 12.

M—He disagrees from all the commentators. He regards BRU 1.2.5 as adhikaraṇa subject matter Ś quotes BRU 1.2.5 in this adhikaraṇa but the Sruti discussed in it is from KATU.. Similarly M holds the view that the present adhikaraṇa does not involve the Ś's doctrine of identity of Brahman and Jīva.

V—He cites and discusses the KATU Śruti in the adhikaraṇa with reference to the interpretation of Brahman and Jīva. According to V the God.is the enjoyer of the fruits.V also quotes the KATU 1.2.18-20 to strengthen his view in the Sūtra viz. attācarācargrahaṇat.

N—In this adhikaraṇa N shows the absence of any experience of pleasure and pain due to karma on the part of Brahman. N regards the Highest Self as eater alone because the terms 'Brāhmaṇa' and 'Kṣatriya' implies 'movable and immovable metaphorically (edible objects—food).

(7) BRS 1.2.11-12.

The adhikaraṇa deals with the KATU 3.1. Ṛtam pibantau....Sukṛtasya loke.....ye ca triṇāciketā in BRS 1.2.11-12.

Ś—The two who have entered in the heart's cavity referred to Brahman and the individual soul for numbrals denote things of the same class. The description of the succeeding passages apply to them only and not to saṁkhyas buddhist and Jīva.

Ś quotes KATU 1.3.3 ātmānam raṭhinam...and 1.3.7 to prove his point.

R—He agrees with Ś in respect of the two viz. 'Brahman and Soul' referred in the Śruti but he contradicts the explanation and remarls on Ś that Ś's explanation is unconvincing and implies prayojaka bhavaḥ i.e. jīva is prayoja while Brahman is prayojaka. R quotes KATU 2.12, 4.7, 1.14 to strengthen his point. R takes this sūtra in the last adhikaraṇa 1.2.10.

M—He introduces the Śruti-KATU 3.1 as similar to Ś's adhikaraṇa consisting its very, as its subject. M refuses to consider Ś and R's interpretations as proper since it does not imply the primary sense of the words. He emphasises that charactery mark, as the enjoyer of fruit of deeds and the use of dual; should be granted in such a way that it would not harm the divine's oneness. He differs from Ś and R and suggests the enjoyers as the two forms of Brahman known as Ātma and the Antarātma or the inner controller.

Ś and R use this adhikaraṇa for the refutation of sāṁkhya while M ciriticises on Ś, R as well as the Sāṁkhyas also.

V—He agrees with Ś and R, regarding the subject matter of the adhikaraṇa but he differs in interpretation of the Śruti. He explains the śruti in the following manner.

The word ṛta denotes to drink svarupāmṛta and that meaning is applicable to both, viz. Brahman and Jīva. The word sukṛta means Brahman (as referred in TU 2.7) according to V. The word chāyā conveys the Jīva it is equal to parabrahman just as the shadow is with the body; similarly the jīva is like Brahman since it attains the sāyujya mokṣa. But Brahman is higher than Jīva; because it has ānanda. That is why he is mentioned by 'ātapa' word in the śruti. The śrutis 1.120, 1.2.16, 1.33, etc. are quoted to strengthen his view by V. This is how the words like chāyatapau, sukṛta etc. are applicable to jīva and Brahman according to the View of V.

N—He explains the adhikaraṇa like Ś and R regarding the entrance of two in the heart viz. Brahman and Jīva because both of them are sentient beings, but he quotes KATU 1.17, 3.2 to elaborate his view that the Śrutis mention the object to be known, and the knower specifically.

(8) BRS 1.3.24.25

The KATU 2.4.12 is referred in the BRS 1.3.24.25.

Ś—He refers KATU 2.4.12 "aṅguṣṭhamātraḥ puruṣ omadhya-ātmani tiṣṭhati and 2.4.13 aṅguṣṭhamātraḥ puruṣo jyotirivā....etodvaitat" in the sūtra Śabdādeva pramitaḥ. MU 2.2.11 is discussed in the adhikaraṇa. The person referred in KATU is Brahman, a ruler of past and present; future. The limitation is size of a thumb and residence in heart can be applicable to Him only. Yama replies the Being of the size of a thumb thus : "that which you wanted to know is this."

R—He takes KATU 2.4.12 as Viṣayavākya of the adhiakraṇa which constitutes sūtras from 23 to 41.

He states that Brahman abides in the heart which is a size of thumb for the sake of worship by the human beings.

M—He refers KATU v.12.14 as a Viṣayvākya which speaks the characteristics of Brahman viz. "Bliss" as eternal, inexhaustible and the highest. "It shines forth only by its grace", is the answer of Yama to Naciketas because all shining forth of things in the world is derived from the Supreme. It is the (His) Light that illumines others, every thought, activity, movement including the flashing forth of Svarūpasukha of Jñānis is but an acting after the activity of the supreme. M puts here the bliss of Jñānis also and argues that it is the subject of same law. It becomes manifested only by the gracious wish of the Lord. The supreme Being is one described as the highest ineffable bliss and the primary source of every form of thought activity and experience including the experience of joy by God-intoxicated souls.

V—V refers this Śrutis while discussing in the Sūtra Śabdādeva Pramitaḥ. He tells that it is this aṅguṣṭhamātraḥ puruṣe which controls the past and future; without the God, no other entity can control it.

N.—1.3.24.

In the BRS 1.3.24 he refers to the KATU 4.12, the Adhikaraṇa deals with the question viz. the Śruti refers to individual soul or the highest person. Brahman is to be meditated on as of the size of merely a thumb. He refers KATU 6.17 to strengthen his point.

(9) The KATU 2.3.2; and 2.3.3 are referred in the BRS 1.3.39.

Ś—The term Prāṇa in the Śruti denotes to Brahman and not vital air because the preceeding and subsequent passages refer to the Brahman. It is in the Prāṇa which is the Brahman, everything tremble. Brahman is responsible for the activities such—burning of fire or Sun's shining. The Śruti speaks attribute of Brahman here.

The KATU 2.3.3 bhayādasyā......pañcamaḥ also proves the same matter.

R—R quotes this Śruti in the Sūtra 1.3.40 viz. "Kampanāt." He refers this passage which comes between aṅguṣṭhamātra puruṣaḥ and aṅguṣṭhamātraḥ puruṣontarārmā. He agrees with Ś's explanation. R and N do not take it as a new section but only resume discussion of section about the person measured as of the size of a thumb.

M—He does not discusses this Śruti under this Sūtra.

V—He begins a new section and discuses how vajra suggests Bhagavānarūpa vajra is only a weapon of Indra because TB 1.1.3 speaks of vajra as agni's heart, it is applied to Bhagavāna it does not state Prāṇa's worship or Indra worship.

N—According to N this Sūtra does not begin the new adhikaraṇa but only resumes the last adhikaraṇa.

He quotes this Śruti in the BRS 1.3.40 'Kampanāt'. The term vital breath in the Śruti denotes the supreme Being because the Lord alone is the cause of trembling the entire universe, produced by Himself. Mahat is also a synonym used for Branman. He concludes that the Śruti declares Him as a cause of fear of all the objects which are enmated in Him. The Lord gives immortality to the knower of Him.

Ś differs in the interpretation. He takes this Sūtra as forming the new adhikaraṇa itself and the Sūtra deals with the question viz. whether the term Prāṇa in KATU 6-2 denotes the Brahman or not.

(10) KATU 1.3.10-11—

Indriyebhyaḥ parāhyarthā.....mahānpar// and mahataḥ paramvyakta.....sā kāṣthā sā parāgatiḥ// are discussed in the BRS 1.4.1-7.

The expression of the words in KATU viz. mahat, avyákta Puruṣa etc. do not include the sāṁkhya doctrine, but they apply to the supreme self.

Ś—Ś utilizes this adhikaraṇa to refute Sāṁkhyas and establishes his view that the whole dicussion is about the Supreme Self in which Naciketas asked Yama three questions only. viz. about the fire, individual soul and the Supreme Self. Pradhāna is mentioned herein. The Śruti 3.10 "the mahat (great) is Superior to the intellect clearly shows it is used in a different sense from the intellect and refer to the Self in reality. The passage under discussion comes after another passage where the simile of chariot is used. The Śruti shows hirarcy among indriya object, mahat etc. avyakta indicate the nature of the highest abode. Ś quotes KATU 1.3.3-4, 1.3.12, 1.1.2, 1.1.5.10, 1.4, 2.1.10, 1.2.22 etc. to point out the difference.

R—R also uses this adhikaraṇa for Sāṁkhyas refutation. He rejects that mahat, avyakta etc. denotes Prakṛti, Pradhāna. R argues that avyakta denotes the body described in chariot simile. R interpretes the adhikaraṇa in different way.

M—M regards this adhikaraṇa containing the Sūtras 1 to 9. The adhikaraṇa establishes harmony in the terms like Avyakta, Jīva, Mahat etc. The term avyakta indicates the supreme Brahman itself which is contained in the principle of avyakta and resides in it. The latter part of the Sūtra 1 refers to Brahman's being present in avyakta which on account of its inferiority of status is treated like a 'body' because M quotes KATU 1.3.3 but also extends to Subāla Up and RU to give witness to the all-pervasive Brahman residing in avyakta (tuccha). He disagrees with Ś and R, in interpretation of avyakta as 'body' because it is gross while avyakta means subtle. Similarly Brahman deserves to be called invisible the attributes denoted by avyakta jīva etc. are controlled by Brahman in the sense that presence in them is deterimined by Its will.

V—He also refutes Sāṁkhyas is this adhikaraṇa since Sāṁkhya doctrine is not vaidic. He differs from Ś and R in interpreting the words avyakta, Bhagavatkṛpā or akṣarbrahma. It implies dharma-dharmi relation like a lamp and its light (Bhagavatkṛpā and Brahaman have relation of this kind.) avyakta is not jñeya, but avyakta is a object (पदार्थ). He agrees with Ś and R in stating the view that the context shows it is the chapter of Brahman and not of Prakrti. He quotes KATU various times merely to strengthen his point viz. 1.1.14 1.1.20, 1.1.22, 1.2.14.1.2.15., 1.3.1, 1.2..22, 1.1.13, 1.1.12, 1.1.16 it is a Naciketa Upākhyana.

N—He refutes the Sāṁkhyas in this Sūtra-that the KATU 3.11 does not establish the Pradhana of the Sāṁkhyas but all the words from the Śruti refers to the Brahman. He agrees with S, R, V in taking the subject matter of the KATU Śruti. He states that the term unmanifest is to be understood in the sense of body which is put down in the similee of the chariot. The text shows the body by stating the mode of subduing the sense organs. In this Śruti, a man who wishes the emancipation, which is the road of the transmigratory existenec, and who is the enjoyer, is the main person who is presented as the lord of the chariot metaphorically, his body which is subordinate to him as the place of his enjoyment is represented as the chariot; the sence organs when controlled by the manas reach the place of the Viṣṇu. The KATU 3.9 and 3.11 denote that nothing is higher that place of the Viṣṇu. The "higher than the great" denotes the superiority of the Supreme Being than the individual soul according to the view of N.

(11) The KATU 1.3.10 is discussed in the BRS 3.3.14-15

The Śruti aims at teaching the Ātman as the superior one than all those mentioned in the passage. The Sūtra refutes the view that the purport of passage is to state of the hi of senses, objects and so on. the Śtuti gives information about them for the sake of meditation; it has purpose which results in the final release. KATU 1.3.15 viz is referred "one is freed from the mouth of death", to strengthen the view.

KATU 1.3.12 is referred in 15th sūtra ātma śabdāt ca for the confirmation of the subject which is explained in the last Sūtra. The enumeration of the series helps to turn the mind towards the Ātman, which is hard to realize without the deep meditation.

R—R refers to TU 11.5 because the Brahman cannot posses a head, wings, tail in reality, it can be said figuratively, it is intended for the purpose of meditation for the sake of easy comprehension.

M—He makes separate Adhikaraṇa of 15 and 16 and the adhikaraṇa determines the upasaṁhāra and anupasaṁhara of attributes in the sense already defined in adhikaraṇa third. He comments on Ś that Ś uses this adhikaraṇa to carry out his found.

V—He does not explain the Śruti. He does not take this as a separate adhikaraṇa.

N—N follows R's interpretation.

(12) The KATU 1.3.1 is discussed in the BRS 3.3.34 ṛtam pibantau sukṛtasyaloke...

also MU—dvā suparṇā sayujā...

The topics deals with the question of two texts, it state different vidyās or one vidyā only.

Ś—The Sūtra states that both the texts describe one vidyā since both mention the Supreme self as existing in the form of individual soul and show the identity of supreme Brahman and individual soul. Both the texts teach the object of meditation as one. So the vidyās are same. Ś refers this Śruti for the second time

R—According to R the Sūtra answers to an objection forward against the conclusion in the last Sūtra. He does not cite KATU in this Sūtra.

M—He does not discuss this Śruti under the very Sūtra. He takes this Sūtra in reply of objection based on the conclusion of the previous Sūtra that there is no restriction in the matter of all Aprokṣajñānins attaining mokṣ.

V—He discusses TU in this Sūtra regarding the attribute of bliss pertaining to last Sūtra.

N—He does not refer KATU in this adhikaraṇa.

(13) KAU and BRS

The BRS deals with the problem of Devayāna in the 4.3.1 to the 4.3.14. It is told that one who knows Saguṇa Brahman, he goes by Devayāna after the death. The Devayāna path is stated differently in the various Ups. as follows : The CHU 8.6.5, 5.10.1.The BRU 6.2.15. The MU 1.2.11, The Praśna Up. 1.10 The KAU 1.3. etc.

Ś quotes the above mentioned Śrutis and discusses the question that if there are various paths or there is only one path having different dharmas by which the knower (K jñāni)

attains Brahmaloka. Ś concludes that Ups. do not mention various paths for attaining the world of Brahman though some of the differences in the Śrutis which they are mentioned in the number of vidyās, i.e. Dahar vidyā; Prāṇa vidyā; Upakosala vidyā etc. The path which leads to Brahmaloka describes various stops but there is only one path because the person who attains Brahmaloka, obtains the same fruit. Ś gives the gradation of the various Śruti which deal with the Devayāna.

The KAU which says that he comes to the world of Vāyu should be placed after the CHU 5.10.1, 2 that means the person reaches to the world of Vāyu after the year (Saṁvatsara) and before the world of Āditya. The Śruti of the BRU 5.10.1 supports to Ś's opinion when it is said the person comes to the world of Vāyu after death, then Vāyu gives him a way just as a "hole of the chariot", by that entrance he goes higher and then to the "Āditya". KAU only mentions that he comes to the Varuṇa, then to the Indra, then to the World of the Prajāpati, but this Up. does not mention the order. According to Ś, "Sa varuṇalokam" of the KAU should be placed after the CHU 4.15.5[5] because there is a connection between the vidyut and the Varuṇa. It is observed that when there is rumbling in the clouds the rain fall. The CHU 7.11.1 describes the same eternal fact[6]. Varuṇa is a god of rain is a well-known fact. After these sentences "Sa Indralokam" "Sa Prajāpatilokam" of the KAU should come in the arcirādimārga according to the view of Ś.

BRS (4.3.1) Arcirādhikaraṇa and BRS (4.3.2) Vāyu adhikaraṇa.

Ś—The Śrutis taken up for the discussion are as follow—The BRU 6.2.15; KAU 1.3; CHU 5.10.1; CHU 5.10.2.

The paths described by the various Ups. are shown below[7] :—

(i) KAU

World of Agni (fire)
↓
World of Vāyu (air)
↓
World of Varuṇa
↓
World of Indra
↓
World of Prajāpati
↓
World of Brahman
↓
Lightening

(ii) CHU

Light
↓
day
↓
Bright half of the month
↓
Six months of the northern path of the Sun (Uttarāyaṇa)
↓
Year
↓
Sun
↓
Moon
↓
Lightening

(iii) BRU

Light
↓
day
↓
Bright half of the month
↓
Six months when the Sun progress to the north Uttarāyaṇa
↓
World of gods
↓
Sun
↓
Lightening

It may be observed from the above mentioned paths, that the Śrutis describe the Devayāna-mārga with addition and deduction. Ś reconciles the various Śrutis from the Ups.

to make Devayāna path complete.[8] So the Devayāna path may be shown fully according to Ś as follows :—

Deity identified with Arcis (rays or light)

↓

day

↓

Bright half of the month (Śuklapakṣa)

↓

Six months of the Sun's progress towards the northern

↓

Year

↓

World of gods

↓

World of Vāyu

↓

Sun

↓

Moon

↓

Lightening

↓

World of Varuṇa

↓

World of Indra

↓

World of Prajāpati

↓

World of Brahman

R—He takes the problem of placing the order of the Śrutus in his Bhāṣya.

R mentions the Devayāna path as follows :—

Light (the world of fire)

↓

day

↓

half month

↓

half year

↓

Year

↓

The World of devas

↓

Vāyu

↓

Sun

↓

Moon

↓

Light

↓

World of Varuṇa

↓

World of Indra

↓

World of Prajāpati

R takes the agniloka as a synonymous with arcis (Light) so he put it at the first.

M—M also handles the problem of reconcilation of the Upaniṣadic Śrutis. He places the order of the various destinations according to its goal which come within the route. He contradicts with all the other ācāryas and states that the soul does not travel by the two paths viz. Devayāna and Pitṛyāna after he passes away. M concerns only one route which begins with the Arcis. The Jñānis travel by this path after Utkranti from their bodies through Brahmanāḍi, is the argument set forth by M. The Arcirādimārga is as follows :—

arci

↓

vāyu (ātivāhika)

↓

day

↓

bright half of the month when the Sun moves northward

↓

Year

↓

Vidyut

↓

Varuṇa

↓

Prajāpati

↓

Moon

↓

Indra

↓

lightening (dyaus bharati)

↓

Vāyu

↓

purusottamam

M criticises on Ś when he places the Varuṇa, Indra etc. after Vidyut. M seems that such a order of places in the path puts in the difficulty viz. It loses the link between the person who leads the 'Knower' to the Brahman and vidyut. (BRS 4.3.5 vaidyutor). He argues that the act of handing over the knower to the hands of Brahman is the one which takes place at the end of the journey and not at some intermediate stage on the journey. Thus M inserts two 'vidyuts' and two vāyu to be reached in the path. He interpretes the Taḍidadhikaraṇa an Vāyugatyadhikaraṇa i.e. 4.3.3, 4.3.2 respectively; distinctly from Ś and R.

The first Vāyu is Ātivāhika and the second vāyu is the mukhya-prāṇa. Similarly the first vidyut is the deity of lightening and the second vidyut is the dyaus Bhārati which takes the man to the Brahman.

M does not consider the vidyut and varuṇa as one and the same stage, like those of Ś and R, because he tells that the lightening is seen because of its lustrous form and not due to its being below the waters. Thus the lightening and Varuṇa both are distinct stations mentioned by the CHU and KAU Śrutis.

V—He does not touch to the question of placing the order of the Śrutis relating to Devayāna.

N—He agrees with Ś and R on the point i.e. to say there is only one path alone which is described through various Śrutis. N reconciles these Śrutis differently from Ś and R.

N discusses the question of removing inconsistancy between the Śrutis and arranges the order of its stages as follows :—

light
↓
bright fortnight
↓
the six months when the Sun goes to the north
↓
year
↓
air
↓
Sun
↓
Moon
↓
Lightening
↓
World of Varuṇa
↓
World of Indra
↓
World of Prajāpati

N identifies the world of gods with the air. Ś does not identify the world of gods with the air but takes them to be the two separate places. R also identifies the world of gods with the air.

Thus the departing soul reaches the Brahman through various stages. The destination mentioned in the Śrutis is the same viz. "Brahmaloka".

(15) 'Prāṇas tathā nu gamāt' BRS 1.1.28 discusses the KAU 3.3.viz. "aṭha khalu Prāṇa eva Prajñātmedam Śarira."

Ś—He takes Prāṇa in the sense of Brahman and not in the sense of breath or the individual soul or the vital air. According to Ś this passage i.e. KAU 3.3 refers to the single type of meditation, the Brahman is the subject matter of the Śruti in the form of its two adjuncts of the individual soul and the life as referred to Indra imparts Pratardana about the supreme one through the words "know me only". Indra preached that His self is identical with the Highest Self.

R—He quotes KAU 3.3 to establish his view that in Viṣ ayavākya viz. 'Sarvam khalu idam brahma' the Paramātman alone is described everyone.

M—He remarks[9] Indra asked Pratardana to worship him who was Prāṇa and Prajñātman. According to him the reference to the Paramātman as in the expression ānandō ajara, amṛta etc. Shows that Indra is not ajara, amaṛta etc. Though Indra tells to worship Him only, that does not mean Indra is Paramātman. The Śruti refers to the Paramātman and He is the Viṣṇu.

N—He cites the KAU 3.2 in the BRS 1.1.29 and suppose that the object mentioned by the term 'vital breath' is the Highest Self because the qualities like highest auspiciousness, endlessness are applicable to the Highest Self. According to him Prāṇa or Indra does not denote the individual soul. The topic deals about the Highest Self alone. N gives very reasonable argument in the support of his view :—It is said that Pratardana requested Indra to give the boon which is beneficial to the mankind. That means he wished for the highest goal of the men. Thereafrer the vital-breath was taught to Pratardana as the object to be worshipped (KAU 3.2).

The adjective beneficial does not apply to anything else except to the attainment of Brahman. Hence the words Indra, Prāṇa and so on were used by Indra with a view to denote the Brahman. By knowing him alone one surpasses the death. There is no other way to salvation.

According to the view of N, the characteristics are mentioned for the sake of teaching the threefoldness of meditation, just as three kinds of meditations on Brahman are referred to viz. TU.2.1,3.6.

R agrees with N on the point that threefold meditation of the Brahman is mentioned in Pratardana vidyā.

It may be observed that the adhikaraṇa 1.1.29 discusses Pratardana vidyā about the Brahman as the supreme one. The ācāryas like Ś, R, N propound their philosophical views and explain the adhikaraṇa. According to them the Indra taught in the KAU 3.1.4 and so on is a different god. Indra is not a very principle of the universe, Indra is not a 'lightening' (meghasthāniya vidyut) as referred in the Rv, Ātman's principles are attached with it. Sātavalekar in the Daivata saṁhitā of the RV emphasises this point clearly with many examples. Indra is Ātman. He is the supreme Being, the ruler of the universe. If the Rgvedic concept is taken into account it clearly shows that Pratardana vidyā do preaches Indra as "Prāṇa+Prajñā=Ātman. The ācāryas goal is different in name, due to least concerning to Indra as Devatā.

KLU 3.3 in the BRS 3.4.20. to p

Ś—quotes the KLU 3.3 in the BRS 3.4.20 to prove that there are no works for the person who is grounded in the Brahman.

The above mentioned Śruti declares that the mendicants whose minds have become purified, and also who have realised i.e. to say which is to be known in the vedānta vākya, such persons are liberated by following the Sannyāsa. The mendicants do not have effect when they renounce all the actions.

Śaṅkarācārya on the Kathopaniṣad

There is no special need to state explanation of the KATU passages since it will be a repetition. Herein the question about the Śaṅkarācārya's commentory on the KATU and the BRS is tried to examine. While reading the Ś-bhāṣ yas on the KATU and BRS one feels some difference in the interpretational and stylistic methology. It is, therefore, purposed to touch it here.

Ś on the KATU and Ś on the BRS could not be considered as one person since there are minute variations in their commentaries. This very question is touched with reference to the passages which are explained and discussed by Ś in the BRS. The BRS mostly deals with the following KATU passages in it[10] : e.g. KATU—1.2.25, 1.3.1.2, 2.4.12-13, 2.3.2, 1.3.10-11, in the BRS 1.29, 1.2.11-12, 1.3.24, 1.3.39, 1.4.1 respectively. The number of passages which are quoted in support of the running arguments, are not dealt with here. It appears from the study of the both the texts, that the method followed by Ś is distinct in the KATU from that of the BRS.

The Ś on the KATU explains the Upaniṣadic text in which some of the words are explained in brief, following the upaniṣadic principles, while Ś on the BRS interprets and discusses the words with arguments. Ś shows how the meaning of the word applies to Brahman, e.g. in the KATU 1.2.25, Ś tells that the "Brāhmaṇa" and "Kṣatriyas" are the Brahman's food and the mṛtyu is just like a upasecana (infusion). Ś explains these words literally in the KATU; while Ś from the BRS shows why the words 'Brāhmaṇa' and 'Kṣatriya' are applied to Brahman. He derives the meaning of the word 'food' from √at to destroy. The words "Brāhmaṇa" and

"Kṣatriya" in the passage implies the "carācara". Thus the passage intends to say that the Brahman destroys the movable and immovable with the help of mṛtyu, so that mṛtyu is called Upasecana.

If the passage KATU 1.2.25 is explained literally the meaning is not clear. There arises a doubt as to what is conveyed by the words "Brāhmaṇa", "Kṣatriya" and "Upasecana" etc. The passage needs to be explained clearly. The manner of interpretation in both the texts also differs. When Ś propounds his teaching, he goes on explaining and discussing certain words. He anticipates the objection and then after he answers them while interpreting the passage. This can be illustrated by the following comments. viz. BRU 4.3.7—कतम आत्मेति योऽयं विज्ञानमयः प्राणेषु हृदन्त ज्योतिः.........
...मृत्योरूपाणि।

W2*hen he comments on this passage he explains the meaning of the words कतम आत्मा in two ways, viz., कतम इति न्यायसूक्ष्मत्ताया दुर्विज्ञेयत्वादुपपद्येन भ्रान्तिः। अथ वा शरीर व्यतिरिक्ते सिद्धेऽपि करणानि सर्वाणि विज्ञानवनरीव, विवेकतः आत्मनोऽनुपलब्धत्वात्, अत्तोऽहं पृच्छामि—कतम आत्मेति, कतमोऽसौ पेटेन्द्रिय प्राण मनःसु, यस्त्चयोक्त आत्मा, येन ज्योतिषास्त इति उक्तम्।

अथ वा योऽयमात्मा त्वयांभिप्रेतो विज्ञानमयः सर्व इमे प्राणा विज्ञानमया इव, एषु प्राणेषु कतम? यथा समुदितेषु ब्राह्मणेषु सर्व इमे तेजस्विनः कतम एक षडङ्गविदिति।।

It may be observed that the Ś on the BRU and Ś of the BRU, there is complete harmony and no discrepancy regarding the methodology of the interpretation. When he explains the BRU passages in the BRU, he has a mastery of the material which he is handling.

There is a difference in methodology style, language etc. in the case of the KATU and the BRS. When Ś discusses the KATU 1.2.1-2, 1.3.1-2 etc. in the BRS he clearly points out how the particular word denotes Brahman and in which sense the word should be taken in that particular passage. In the "Guhā pravi ṣṭadhikaraṇa" (BRS 1.2.11-12) Ś comments, कस्मात् आत्मानौ हि तावुभावपि चेतनौ समान स्वभावौ... when he concludes the dual in "Pibantau", "Chayatapau" conveys the Jīva and Paramātman and not the Buddhi and Jīva. In this argument the चेतनत्व of both the elements (viz. Jīva and Brahman) is more important. While in the KATU, such explanations on the passages are not found e.g. Ś explains the KATU passage in the following way:—कर्मफलं पिबन्तौ, एकस्तत्र कर्मफलं पिबति भुङ्क्ते नेतरः...

It cannot be claimed that the Ś on the KATU and Ś on the BRS (on the relevant Up.) does not agree in their teaching. No doubt, the Ś on the BRS and Ś on the KATU follows the doctrines stated by the Ups. but the style, usage of the words methodology create a little doubt regarding the authorship. It gives rise to suspect two different persons, though the final conclusions drawn in both the texts are identical. Further it can be said that the conclusions should be identical because even if there are two Śaṅkarācāryas, both of them belong to the same philosophical tradition. They must propound one and the same doctrine.

This section acquaints with the doctrines stated in the BRS, in their simple form, avoiding the complicated references and discussions which are put forth by the ācāryas. It is not claimed that the section contains everything which consists in the BRS but it is tried to give main philosophical tendencies and thoughts, on the basis of the commentaries by the five ācāryas which are presented in the BRS. The BRS is a systematic work on the Ups. and the commentators try to discover the views which are suitable to their philosophical schools. They split the words, passages, suitable to their schools.

Similarly if the ācārya follows the Upaniṣadic thought or he does not follow it, may be observed from their comments noted in the relevant passages.

At the end one may conclude the present research work with the prayer :—

"Om Pūrṇamadaḥ Pūrṇamidam
Pūrṇat Pūrṇamudacyate
Pūrnasya Pūrṇamādāta Pūrṇamevāvaśiṣyate."
Om, Śāntiḥ Śāntiḥ Śāntiḥ.

REFERENCES

1. The dates of the five ācāryas are following to the Radhakrishanan S. The Brahma-sūtra (The philosophy of spiritual life).
2. नागुरतछ्रुतेरिति चेन्नेतरराधिकारात्। BRS 2.3.21.
3. BRS 3.2.1 "Sandhyesrṣtirāhs".
4. BRS 2.3.18.
5. CHU 4.15.5.
6. CHU 7.11.1.
7. vide Bhatakhande S.M. : The Chandogya Upanishad and the Brahmasutras (a comparative study) p. 31-33.
8. For more details vide BRS SBH on BRS 4.3.1, BRS 4.3.2 and also Bhatakhande S.M. "The Chandogya Upanishad and the Brahmasutras." (A Comparative Study).
9. "अत्रापि प्राणो विष्णुरेव, तं देवाः प्राणयन्तः इत्याधनुगमात्"।
10. The KATU passages are illustrated in the Appendix No. 2.

APPENDIX NO.1

CHU 5.3.6, 5.9.1 and B RU 6.2.9.11.

(1) CHU

असौ वाव लोको गौतमाग्नितस्यादित्य एव समिद्रश्मये।
धूमोऽहरर्चिश्चन्द्रमा अङ्गारा नक्षत्राणि विस्फुल्लिङ्गाः।।

(1) BRU

असौ वै लोकोऽग्नि गौतम तस्यादित्य एव समिद्रश्मयो
धूमोऽहरर्चि दिशोऽङ्गारा अवान्तर-दिशो विस्फुल्लिङ्गः।।

In the CHU the candramas (moon) is the aṅgāra (coal) and nakṣatras (stars) are sparks (visphuliṅgas) while in the BRU the dik is called the aṅgāra and the avāntare dik-s (intermediate quarters) are sparks.

In both the Ups. असौ वै लोको is a common factor with a slight difference of वै and वा. वै/वा are variants.

(2) CHU

पर्जन्यो वाव गौतमाग्निस्तस्य वायुरेव समिदभ्रं धूमो।
विद्युदर्चिरशनिरङ्गारा ह्रादुनयो विस्फुलिङ्गाः।।
तस्मिन्नेतस्मिन्नग्नौ देवाः सोम ँ राजानं जुह्वति।
तस्या आहुतेर्वर्षं ँ सम्भवति।।

(2) BRU

पर्जन्योवाग्निगौतम तस्य संवत्सर एव समिदभ्राणि।
धूमो विद्युदर्चिरशनिरङ्गारा ह्रादुनयो विस्फुलिङ्गाः।।
तस्मिन्नेतस्मिन्नग्नौ देवाः सोम ँ राजानं जुह्वति।
तस्या आहुत्यै वृष्टिः संभवति।।

In the CHU the vāyu is a samit of the Parjanya-fire while in the BRU the fire has samvastsara (year) as the samit. The vocables वर्षा and वृष्टि are synonyms for 'rain'.

(3) CHU

पृथिवी वाव गौतमाग्नितस्याः संवत्सर एव समिदाकाशो।
धूमो रात्रिरर्चि दिंशोऽङ्गारा अवान्तर दिशो विस्फुलिङ्गाः।।
तस्मिन्नेतस्मिन्नग्नौ देवाः वर्षं जुह्वति। तस्या आहुतेरन्नं ॅ संभवति।।

(3) BRU

अयं वै लोकोऽग्निर्गौतम तस्य पृथिव्येव समिदग्नि र्धूमो।
रात्रिरर्चिश्चन्द्रमा अङ्गारा नक्षत्राणि विस्फुलिङ्गाः।।
स्तस्मिन्नेतस्मिन्नग्नौ देवाः वृष्टिं जुह्वति तस्या आहुत्या अन्नं ॅ संभवति।।

The CHU expressly states Pṛthvi as the third fire while the BRU points out the third fire by the words "अयं वै लोकाः"।

The CHU states the samvatsara as the samit while the BRU regards the Pṛthvi as the samit.

In the CHU, dik is aṅgāra, avāntara-dik-s are sparks while in the BRU candramas is aṅgāra and the nakṣatras are visphuliṅgāḥ (sparks). Thus it may be said that the order of the constituents is changed between the first fire i.e. heaven and the third fire i.e. earth.

(4) CHU

पुरुषो वाव गौतमाग्नितस्य वागेव समित्प्राणो धूमो-
जिह्वाऽर्चिश्चक्षुरङ्गारा श्रोत्रं विस्फुलिङ्गाः।।

(4) BRU

पुरुषो वाग्निर्गौतम तस्य व्यात्तमेव समित्प्राणो धूमो-
वागर्चिश्चक्षुरङ्गाराः श्रोत्रं विस्फुलिङ्गाः।।

In the CHU vāk is samit, while in the BRU vyātta

(open mouth) is samit. The CHU states the tongue as a flame, while in the BRU vāk is flame. Here it is tobe noticed that the order of the word changes.

(5) CHU

योषा वाव गौतमाग्निस्तस्या उपस्थ एव समिधदुपमन्त्रयेतसधूमो-
योनिरर्चिर्यदन्तः करोति तेऽङ्गारा अभिनन्दा विस्फुलिङ्गाः॥

(5) BRU

योषा वा अग्निर्गौतम तस्या उपस्थ एव समिल्लोमानि धूमो
योनिरर्चिर्यदन्तः करोति तेऽङ्गारा अभिनन्दा विस्फुलिङ्गाः॥

The CHU states upamantraṇa as the smoke while the BRU states 'Lom' (cohabitation) as the smoke about the fifth fire e.g. yoṣā (woman).

In these five fires the oblations are offered. Jaivali connects the Śraddha libation with the soma, the soma with the rain, the rain with the food, the food with the seed, and finally the seed with the man. Thus the man takes birth after the fifth oblation.

APPENDIX NO. 2

ART'S

यस्य ब्रह्म च क्षत्रं च उभे भवतः ओदनः।
मृत्युर्यस्योपसेचनं क इत्या वेद यत्र सः।। (KATU 1.2.25)
ऋतं पिबन्तौ सुकृतस्य लोके, गुहां प्रविष्टौ परमे परार्धे।
छायातपौ ब्रह्मविदो वदन्ति, पञ्चाग्नयो ये च त्रिणाचिकेता।।
(KATU 1.3.1)
आत्मनः रथिनं विद्धि शरीर ः रथमेव तु।
वुद्धिं तु सारथिं विद्धि मनः प्रग्रहमेव च।। (KATU 1.3.2)
अङ्गुष्ठमात्रः पुरुषो ज्योतिरिवाधूमक।
ईशानो भूतभव्यस्य स एवाध स उश्च।। (KATU 2.4.15)
यदिदं किं च जगत्सर्वं प्राण एजति निःसृतम्।
महद्भयं वज्रमुधतं य एतद्विदुरमृतास्ते भवन्ति।। (KATU 2.3.2)
महतः परमव्यक्त मव्यक्तात्पुरुषः परः।
पुरुषान्न परं किंचित्सा काष्ठा सा परा गतिः।। (KATU 1.3.11)
इंद्रियेभ्यः परा हयर्था अर्थेभ्यश्च परं मनः।
मनस्तु परा बुद्धिर्बुद्धेरात्मा महान्परः।। (KATU 1.3.10)

BIBLIOGRAPHY

General Works

1. Abhyankar and Candorkar, *Brahma Sūtra Śāṅkar-bhāṣya,* Bhandarkar Oriental House, Poona, Pub. Deccan Education Society, Poona 1957.
2. Apte, V.M., *Brahma Sūtra Śāṅkarbhāṣya,* Popular Book Depot.
3. Arya, K. Narayan Swami, *Thirty Minor Upaniṣads,* Pub. Arkay Book Corporation, Delhi 1979.
4. Arora, Udai Prakash, *Motif in Indra Mythology,* Indika Puplishing House, New Delhi 1981.
5. Ayyangar, T.R., *The Vaiṣṇava Upaniṣads,* Adyar Liberary, Madras 1945.
6. Ayyangar, T.R., *The Yoga Upaniṣads,* The Adyar Library, Madras 1952.
7. Bapat D.G., *Aitareya Brāhmaṇa* (Marathi), Parts I, II and III, Satara 1963.
8. Barau—*A History of pre-Buddhistic Indian Philosophy,* Motilal Banarsidass, Delhi (1st rep.) 1970.
9. Belvalkar, S.K. and Ranade, R.D., *History of Indian Philosophy* (Creative Period) Vol. II, Bilvakunja Publishing House, (First Editor) Poona 1927.
10. Belvalkar S.K. (ed. & translated), *Shrimad Bhagvadgita* Vol. I, (Gen. ed.) V.S. Agrawal, Hindu Vishvavidyalaya Nepal Rajya Sanskrit Series, Vol. I, 1959.
11. Benjamin Solis, *Krishna Cycles in the Purāṇas,* Motilal Banarsidass, Delhi 1984.

12. Bhandarkar, R.G., *Vaisnavism, Saivism & Minor Religious Systems,* Indological Book House, Varanasi 1965.
13. Bhanu, C.S., *Katha Upaniṣad with Commentary & Notes of Śāṅkar, Raṅgarāmānuja, Ānandtirtha & Bhimasharma,* Pub. by Damodar Sāvalarāma and Company, Poona 1912.
14. Bhatkhande, S.M., *The Chandogya Upaniṣad and the Brahmasūtras of Bādarāyaṇa,* (A Creative Study), Pub. University of Bombay, Bombay 1982.
15. Bhavabhūti, *Mālatī-Mādhava* with the Comm. of Rasamanjari, Pub. M.M. K.S. Mahadevasastri, Trivandrum Skt. Series No. 170, 1953.
16. Bhavabhūti, *Uttararāma-Caritam,* (Ed.) Bhat, G.K., The Popular Publishing House, Surat, 1965.
17. Bose, Rama—*Vedānta Kaustubha and Vedānta Pārijāta Saurabh* with Brahmasūtra Nimbārka's Commentary, Pub. The Royal Asiatic Society of Bengal, Culcutta, 1941.
18. Burrow, T., *The Sanskrit Language,* Feber and Feber, London 1973.
19. Chatterjee, Chinmoy, *Vedantic Education,* Pub. Gauranga Cultural Research Institute, Jyoti Kunja, Lucknow 1957.
20. Chidbhavananda (Swami), *Bhagvad-Gītā,* Śri Ramkṛṣṇa Tapovaram, 1982.
21. Chinmayananda, *Discourses on Māndūkya Upaniṣad with Gauḍpāda Kārikā,* ed. by K. Annadhanam, 4, Kashmere Gate, Delhi, Second ed. 1958 (During the 91 Gyanayajna).
22. Citrava Siddheshwarashastri, *Pracin Caritrakosha* (Marathi), Pub. Bharatvarshiya Caritrakosh Mandal, Poona 1952.
23. Dandekar, R.N., *Vedic Bibliography,* Vol. I, II, III, Bhandārkar Oriental Research Institute, Poona 1973.

24. Dandekar, R.N., *Vedic Mythological Tracts* (Select Writing-I), Ajanta Publications, Delhi 1979.
25. Dange, S.A., *Legends in the Mahābhārata,* Motilal Banarsidass, Delhi, 1969.
26. Das, Gupta, *History of Indian Philosophy,* Cambridge At the University Press 1940.
27. Deussen, Paul, (Tra. from German by V.M. Bedekar & Palsule, G.B.), *Sixty Upaniṣads of the Veda,* Vols. I & II, Pub. Motilal Banarsidass, Delhi, 1980.
28. Dikshitar, V.R.R., *Purāṇa Index,* Vols. I, II, III, University of Madras, 1955.
29. Diwakar, R.R., *Upaniṣads in Story and Dialogue,* Bharatiya Vidya Bhavan, Bombay, 1964.
30. Moor, Edward, *Hindu Pantheon,* J. Higginbotham Law Book Sellers & Publishers, Calcutta, 1864.
31. Eggeling, Julius, *Śatapatha-Brāhmaṇa,* SBE, Vol. 44, Oxford, Motilal Banarasidass (reprint), Delhi 1963.
32. Gajendragadkar, P.B., *The Ten Classical Upanishads,* Vol. I, Bharatiya Vidya Bhavan, Bombay, 1981.
33. Gambhirananda Swami, *The Brāhamasūtra Śāṅkar-bhāśya,* Advaita Ashrama, Entally Road, Calcutta, 1958.
34. Geldner Karl, F., *Der Rigveda,* Vol. I, II & III, Hos Vol. 33, 34, 35, Cambridge, Musscheselts, Harvard University Press, 1951, 1955,1958.
35. Gough, Edward, *Philosophy of the Upanishadas* (Ancient Indian Metaphysics), Cosmo Publication, New Delhi (3rd reprint) 1979.
36. Griffith, R., *The Hymns of the Rigveda,* Vol. I and II. Chaukhamba Sanskrit Series, No. XXXV, 1950, 1963.
37. Haryappa, H.L., *Legends through the Ages,* Deccan College Series No. 8, Deccan College, Poona, 1953.
38. Jacob, G.A., *A Concordance to the Principal Upaniṣads & Bhagavadgītā,* Motilal Banarasidass, Delhi, 1963.

39. Jog, D.V., *Vaidic Śāṅkarbhāṣya, Advaitamatanuvada* (Marathi), Pub. Balkrishna L. Pathak, Bookseller and Publishers, Bombay, 1954.
40. Joshi, H.S., *Origin and Development of Dattatreya worship in India,* (Thesis), M.S. University, Baroda, 1955.
41. Kālidāsa, *Abhijñāna Śākuntalam* (Ed.) R.D. Karmarkar, Aryabhusana Press, Poona, 1952.
42. Kālidāsa, *Kumāra Saṁbhava* (ed. by) Kale M.R. with the Commentary Mallinath, Pub. Messers Gopal Narayana & Co., Kalbadevi Road, Bombay.
43. Kālidāsa, *Raghuvaṁśam.*
44. Kane, P.V., HDS., Vol. II, V, Part II and IV, Bhandarkar Oriental Research Institute, Poona 1941, 1953, 1962.
45. Kansara, N.M., *Sambodhi,* Vol. 10, No. 1-4., Jan.-April, 1982, Pub. L.D. Institute of Indology, Allahabad.
46. Kantawala, S.G., *The Cultural History from the Matsya Purāṇa* (Thesis), M.S. University of Baroda, Baroda, 1964.
47. Karmarkar, R.D., *Śri-Bhāṣya,* Vol. I, II and III, University of Poona, Sanskrit and Prakrit Series, Vol. I, Poona, 1964.
48. Keith, A.B., *Black Yajurveda,* Hos. Vols. 18 and 19, Cambridge, Massachusetts, The Harvard University Press, 1914.
49. Keith, A.A., *The Religion and Philosophy of Veda and Upanishadas,* Hos No. 31, London, 1925.
50. Keith, A.B., *Rigveda Brāhmaṇas,* Hos. No. 25, 1920.
51. Kolangade, R.G., *Ṛṣi darśana* (Marathi), Yogishwar Prakashan No. 6, (Under Bombay University), Bombay, 1954.
52. Law, B.C., *Historical Geography of the Ancient India,* Pub. Societe Asiatique De Paris, Paris, France, 1954.

53. Limaye, V.P. and Vadekar, R.D. (Ed.), *The Eighteen, Principal Upanishad,s* Tilak Maharashtra Vidya Pith, Vaidic Samshodhan Mandal, Poona, 1958.

54. Macdonell, A.A. and Keith A.B., *Vedic Index of Names and Subjects,* Vol. I and II, Motilal Banarsidass, Varanasi, 1958.

55. Macdonell, A.A., *Vedic Mythology,* Motilal Banarsidass, (reprint), Delhi, 1981.

56. Madhva, *Bṛhadāraṇyaka Upaniṣad,* SBH, Vol. XIV, The Panini Office, Bhuvaneshwari Ashrama, Allahabad, 1909.

57. Madhva, *Chāndogya Upaniṣad,* SBH, Series, The Panini Office, Bhuvaneshwari Ashrama, Allahabad, 1909.

58. Madhvānanda Swami, *Bṛhadāraṇyaka Upaniṣad,* Advaita Ashram Mayavali, Almora, Himalayas, 1950.

59. Mahadevan, T.M.P., *Gauḍapādakārika,* Pub. University of Madras, Madras,1954.

60. Mookerjee, Radha Kumud, *Ancient Indian Education,* Pub. Macmillan and Co. Ltd., St. Martins Street, London, 1947.

61. Nimbārka, *Brahmasūtras,* Kashi Sanskrit SeriesNo. 99, Pub. Chowkhamba Sanskrit Series Office, Benares, 1932.

62. Oldenberg, H., *Hymns to Agni* (I-V maṇḍalas) SBE, Vol. XLVI (ed.) Max Müller, Oxford, 1897.

63. Ortel, H., *The Jaiminiya or Talavakar Upaniṣad Brāhmaṇa,* (From the Journal of the American Oriental Society, Vol. XVI, Part I, 1894), New Hoven, Yale University.

64. Pargiter, F.E., *Ancient Indian Historical Tradition,* Motilal Banarsidass, Delhi, 1962.

65. Pusalkar, A.D., *Studies in Epics and Purāṇas of India,* Bharatiya Vidya Bhavan, Bombay, 1955.

66. Radhakrishnan, S., *Bhagavad Gītā,* George Allen and Unwin Ltd., London, (2nd Imp.) 1949.
67. Radhakrishnan, S., *The Brahmasūtras* (The Philosophy of Spiritual Life), Ruskin House, George Allen & Urwin Ltd. London (Second Impression), 1971.
68. Radhakrishnan, S., *The Principal of Upaniṣads,* George Allen & Urwin Ltd. London, 1953.
69. Ranade, R.D., *Constructive Survey of Upaniṣadic Philosophy,* 1926, Oriental Book Agency, Poona, 1926.
70. Raghunathan, N., *Śrīmad-Bhāgavatam,* Vol. I and II, Vighneswara Publishing House, Madras, 1976.
71. Raṅga Rāmānujācārya, *Bṛhadāraṇyaka Upaniṣad,* Ass. No. 64, Poona, 1911.
72. Raṅga Rāmānuja, *Chandogya Upaniṣad,* Anandashram, Ed. No. 63, 1916, Ass. No. 63, Poona, 1910.
73. Roer, G., *The Twelve Principal Upaniṣads,* Vol. I, II & III, Nag Publications, Delhi, 1979.
74. Roy, Pratapchandra, (Ed.) Hiralal Haldar (Vol. III) (2nd ed.), *The Mahābhārata,* Oriental Publishing Co., Culcutta 1954.
75. *Śaṅkara Brahmasūtra,* (Śāṅkarabhāṣya), Pub. Nirnayasagar Press, Bombay, 1927.
76. Śaṅkarācārya, Bṛhadāraṇyaka Upaniṣad, Geeta Press, Gorakhpur, 1958.
77. Śaṅkarānanda, *Kauṣitaki Upaniṣad,* SBH, Vol. XXXI Part I, Allahabad.
78. Śaṅkarānanda, S., *Maitri Upaniṣad* SBH Vol. XXXI, Part 2, Published by Major B.D. Basu, Basu, Bhuvaneswari Aśram, Allahabad.
79. Satavalekar, D.V., *Agni Suktonkā manana,* Svādhyāya Mandala, Pardi, 1880.
80. Satyaprakash Swami, *Parables and Dialogues From the Upaniṣads,* S. Chand & Co. (Pvt.), Ltd., Delhi, 1975.

81. Sauch, G. Gispert, *Bliss in the Upanishads,* Pub. World's Wisdom Series No. 2, Delhi, 1977.

82. Shah, J.G. (Guj.), *Brahamasūtra Aṇubhāṣya,* Pub. Shri A.A. Bhatt, Bhavanagar, 1981.

83. Shah, J.G., *Śrimad Vallabhācārya, His Philosophy and Religion,* Pushtimārgiya Pustakalaya Nadiada, 1969.

84. Sharma, Baldev Raj, *The Concept of Ātman & The Principal Upaniṣads,* Dinesh Publications, New Delhi, 1972.

85. Sharma, B.N.K., *Brahmasūtras and The Principal Commentators of Brahmasūtras,* Bharatiya Vidya Bhavan, Vol. I, II, III, Bombay, 1971, 74, 76.

86. Sharma, T.R., *Studies The Sectarian Upaniṣads,* Indological Book House, Varanasi, 1972.

87. Shastri, Badrinath, *Vāyu Purāṇa,* Baroda, 1914.

88. Shastri, V.B., *Vaidika Padānukramakośa,* Vol. II, The Śāntakuti Vedic Series (Viśnabandhu Śāśtri), Lahore, 1936.

89. Shende, N.J., *The Religion and Philosophy of the Atharvaveda,* Bhandarkar Oriental Series No. 8, Poona, 1952.

90. Upadhyaya, Baldeva, *Purāṇa Vimarsha,* The Chowkhamba Vidya Bhavan, Varanasi, 1955.

91. Vallabha, *Brahmasūtrānubhāṣyaya*, Pub. Nirnayasagar Press, Bombay,

92. Vettam Mani, *Purāṇic Encylopaedia,* Motilal Banarasidass (4th ed.), 1974.

93. Whitney W.D. and Lanman, C.R. (Trans.), *The Atharvaveda,* Part I and II, Hos. Vol. 7 and 8, Cambridge Massachusetts, Harvard University, 1905.

94. Wilson, H.H., *Viṣṇu Purāṇa* (A System of Hindu Mythology and Tradition), Punthis Pustak, Calcutta, 1961.

95. Winternitz, M., *A History of Indian Literature,* Vol. I. (Translated from the Original German By M.S. Ketkar), University of Calcutta, 1927.

Original Works

1. *A Grammatical Word Index to Atharvaveda,* (Both recensions), ed. VVRI, Hoshiarpur, 1963.
2. *Aitreya Āraṇyaka,* Ass. No. 38, Poona, 1898.
3. *Aitareya Brāhmaṇa* With Sāyaṇa's Commentary, ASS. No. 32, Poona, 1896.
4. *Bhāgavata Mahā Pūrāṇa,* (ed.) Shastri Rama Teja, Laxminārāyaṇa Press, Benares, 1952.
5. *(Professor) Birinch Kumar Barua Commemoration Volume,* All India Oriental Conference, Gauhati. 1966.
6. *Brahmanic Citations,* VVRI, Hoshiarpur, 1966.
7. *Brahmāṇḍa Purāṇa* (ed.), Shastri, J.L., Pub. Motilal Banarasidass, Delhi, 1973.
8. *Encyclopaedia of Britannica* Vol. 3, Pub. Helen Hemingway Benton, 1973-74.
9. *Jaiminīya, Brāhmaṇa,* (ed.) Raghuvir and Lokesh Sharma, Sarasvati Vihara Series Vol. 21, 1950.
10. *JUB,* Vol. XIX (new series) Part 2, Sept. 1950, University of Bombay, Bombay.
11. *JUB,* Sept. Part 2, 1959, University of Bombay, Bombay.
12. *JUB,* Sept. Part 2, 1960, University of Bombay, Bombay.
13. *JUB,* Vol. XXXI—Part 2, 1962, University of Bombay, Bombay.
14. *JUB,* Sept. Part II, 1963, University of Bombay, Bombay.
15. *Journal of the Ganganath Jha Research Institute,* Vol. 3, Part II, Nov. 1945, Allahabad.
16. *Journal of the Royal Asiatic Society,* London, 1973.

17. *Kalyāṇa,* Vol. No. 31, (Tirthaṅka), Geeta Press, Gorakhpur, 1957.
18. *Kalyāṇa,* Vol. No. 23, (Upaniṣadaṅka), Geeta Press, Gorakhpur, 1948.
19. *Kalyana Kalpataru,* Vol. 27, July, 1963.
20. *Kauṣitaki Brāhmaṇa* text, (ed.) Heradsgegebenvon, E.K. Sreekrishna Sarma, Franz Steiner Verlag Gmbh, Uicsbaden, 1968.
21. *Kapiṣthalakōṣṭha Saṁhitā,* (ed.) Raghuvir, Pub. Meherchand Lachhmandas Sanskrit Depot, Lahore, 1932.
22. *Life Beyond Magazine,* Vol. III. N. 5, Feb. 1983.
23. *Ludwick Sternbuch Felicitation Volume,* Akhila Bharatiya Sanskrit Parishad, Lucknow, 1979.
24. *Mahābhārata,* (Critical ed.), Bhandarkar Oriental Research Institute, Poona.
25. *Mahābhārata,* Geeta Press, Gorakhpur.
26. *Manu Smṛti* with Kulluka's Commentary (6th ed.) Pub. Pandurang Jawaji, Nirnaya Sagar Press, Bombay, 1920.
27. *Nāradiya Purāṇa,* Nag Publishers, 1984.
28. *Matsya Purāṇa,* ASS, No. 54, Poona, 1907.
29. *Matsya Purāṇa* Vol. I and Vol. II. (ed.) Jamna Das Akhtar, The Sacred Books of the Aryans Series. Oriental Publishers, Delhi, 1972.
30. *Pañchavimśa Brāhmaṇa.*
31. *Prabudha Bharati,* January-December, 1941, Calcutta.
32. *Proceedings and Transactions of the Third Oriental Conference Madras,* December, 1924. Printed The Law Printing House, Madras, 1925.
33. *Ṛgveda Maṇḍalas 1 to 10,* with Sāyaṇa's Commentary, Pub. Tilak Maharashtra Vidyapitha, Vaidik Saṁsodhana Maṇḍala, Poona, 1933, 1936, 1941, 1946.

34. *Ṛgvedic Maṇḍalas 1 to 10,* With the Commentaries of Skandaswāmin, Udgitha, Veṅkatamādhava, and Mudgala (ed.) by VVRI, Hoshiarpur, 1963, 1965, 1964, 1966.

35. *The Samnyāsa Upaniṣads,* With the Upaniṣad Brahmayogin Commentary ed. by Dikashitar, T.R.C., The Adyar Library and Research Centre (reprint), Vol. 12, Madras, 1966.

36. *The Śākta Upaniṣads* with Brahmayogin's Comm. (ed.) Mahadeva Sastri, The Adyar Library and Research Centre No. 10, Madras, 1950.

37. *The Śaiva Upaniṣads* with Brahmayogin's Comm. (ed.) Mahadeva Shastri, The Adyar Library Series, No. 9, Madras, 1950.

38. *Śatapatha Brāhmaṇa* with Sāyaṇa, Kavirāj Saraswati & Hariswami's Commentary, Laxmivyamkateshvar Stream Press, Kalyana, Bombay, 1940.

39. *Taittiriya Brāhmaṇa,* ASS. No. 36, Poona, 1897.

40. *Taittiriya Brāhmaṇa,* ASS. No. 37, Poona, 1898.

41. *Taittiriya Brāhmaṇa*, ASS. No. 42, Poona, 1901.

42. *Tāṇḍyamahābrāhmaṇa,* Kashi Sanskrit Series No. 105, Banaras, 1936.

43. *The Upaniṣads,* (ed. & Translated) Max Müller, Pub. by SBE Vol. 25, Part I & Part II, (reprint) Motilal Banarasi-dass, Delhi, 1981.

44. *The Ten Principal Upaniṣads* with Śāṅkarbhāṣya, Pub. Motilal Banarsidass, Delhi, 1978 (Reprint).

45. *The Unpublished Upaniṣads* (ed.) The Pandits of Adyar Liberary Under C. Kunjar Raja, Madras, 1933.

46. *Vaidika Padānukramakoṣa,* VVRI, S.V. Series, Vol. XIII, Hoshiarpur, 1962.

47. *Varāha Purāṇa,* All India Kashiraj Trust, Varanasi, 1981.

48. *Vedanta Kesari,* May, 1963.

49. *Viṣṇu Purāṇa,* Oriental Press, Bombay, 1899.

50. *Viṣṇu Purāṇa,* Geeta Press, Gorakhpur.

51. *The Yoga Upaniṣads* with Brahmayogin's Commentary (ed.) Mahadeva Shastri, The Adyar Library Series, Vol. 6, The Adyar Library (Reprint), Madras, 1968.

☆☆☆

INDEX

A

H

I

J

K

T

☆☆☆